Botanicum

To Charlotte and Donald—for their part in nurturing my love of plants
K. S.

For all budding plant and fungal scientists
K. W.

Text copyright © 2016 by Kathy Willis
Design copyright © 2016 by The Templar Company Limited
Illustrations copyright © 2016 by Katie Scott
Designed by Winsome d'Abreu
Edited by Katie Haworth

First U.S. edition 2017

Library of Congress Catalog Card Number pending
ISBN 978-0-7636-8923-0

16 17 18 19 20 21 RDS 10 9 8 7 6 5 4 3 2 1

Printed in Shenzhen, Guangdong, China

This book was typeset in Gill Sans and Mrs Green.
The illustrations were created with pen and ink and colored digitally.

BIG PICTURE PRESS
an imprint of
Candlewick Press
99 Dover Street
Somerville, Massachusetts 02144

www.candlewick.com

This book was produced in consultation with plant and fungal experts at the
Royal Botanic Gardens, Kew. With thanks to Bill Baker, Paul Cannon, Mark Chase,
Martin Cheek, Colin Clubbe, Phil Cribb, Aljos Farjon, Lauren Gardiner, Olwen Grace, Aurélie Grall,
Tony Kirkham, Bente Klitgaard, Carlos Magdalena, Mark Nesbitt, Rosemary Newton, Lisa Porkny,
Martyn Rix, Paula Rudall, Dave Simpson, Rhian Smith Wolfgang Stuppy, Anna Trias-Blasi,
Jonathan Timberlake, Tim Utteridge, Maria Vorontsova, Jurriaan de Vos, James Wearn, Paul Wilkin.

With special thanks to Gina Fullerlove, Kew Publishing, and Emma Tredwell, Kew Digital Media.

Welcome to the Museum · ENTER HERE

Botanicum

illustrated by KATIE SCOTT

written by KATHY WILLIS

BPP

Preface

Plants are everywhere. They live on almost every surface on Earth, from the highest mountains to the lowest valleys, from the coldest and driest environments to some of the hottest and wettest places on our planet.

Vast numbers of plants live in water—in oceans, lakes, rivers, and swamps—in conditions ranging from extreme salinity (saltiness) to fresh, fast-flowing rivers. The smallest plants are tiny, single-celled microscopic organisms less than 0.001 millimeters across. They are so small that you'd need about a hundred of them to make up the size of a grain of sand. The tallest are huge trees, towering more than 260 feet/80 meters, as tall as a twenty-six-story building.

Nobody knows for certain how many species of plants there are. So far, scientists have counted about 425,000, but more are being discovered every day. There are clear patterns as to where on Earth plants thrive best, and the conditions they need. In the hot, wet tropics, for example, there are more than eighty species of trees for every $2\frac{1}{2}$ acres/1 hectare; at the cold, arid North and South Poles, there are fewer than eight. Understanding these patterns of plant diversity is crucial to preserving all other forms of life on Earth, including us. Because without plants, there would be no humans. Plants create and regulate the air we breathe, and they provide us with food, medicines, textiles to make our clothes, and materials to build our homes. So how do they do it? How did all this happen? How did Earth reach the diversity and variety of plant life we see around us today? What did the first plants look like? When did the first forests form? When did plants first produce flowers? What are the biggest, smallest, weirdest, rarest, ugliest, and smelliest plants on Earth? Wander through this museum and all will be revealed.

Professor Kathy Willis
Royal Botanic Gardens, Kew, London, England

Welcome to Botanicum

This is no ordinary museum. Imagine if you could wander through every field, wood, tropical rain forest, and flower glade in the world. Think what it would be like if you could see the most beautiful, exotic, and weird plants all at once. Have you ever wondered what you would see if you could stroll back in time, to the beginnings of life on Earth? You can, in the pages of *Botanicum*.

Tour the galleries and learn how plants have been around many millions of years longer than us. Find out about plants that have changed over time, and about others that have stayed the same. Stroll through our exhibits and discover the many different life-forms of plants.

Look carefully—some of the plants you'll see here can also be found in your garden or local park. Many of the plants in our galleries may also be in your kitchen cupboard—did you know you eat plants from the grass family, probably every day?

You will learn some fascinating science, such as why some plants are green and others are not. How some plants live in water and others are suspended in midair, not connected to the ground at all. And even how some plants feed on flesh. Plants are some of the biggest, smallest, oldest, and smelliest forms of life on Earth.

Enter *Botanicum* and discover the strange and wonderful kingdom of plants, in all its colorful, surprising majesty.

Mulberries

Oaks

Squashes

Cabbages

Wood sorrels

Legumes

Eucalyptuses

Geraniums

Spider lilies

Passion vines

Bananas

Orchids

Palms

Bromeliads

Grasses

Lilies

Grapevines

Pandans

Yams

Pondweeds

EUDICOTS

MONOCOTS

Laurels

Magnolias

Amborellas

Nymphaeales

Horsetails

Black peppers

ANGIOSPERMS

SEED PLANTS

Whisk ferns

FERNS

Club mosses

VASCULAR PLANTS

Red algae

Leptosporangiate ferns

Single-celled algae

LAND PLANTS

Hibiscuses

Honeysuckles

Sunflowers

Carrots

Snapdragons

Potatoes

Maples

Hollies

Forget-me-nots

Saxifragales

Dogwoods

ASTERIDS

Rhododendrons

ROSIDS

Gunnerales

Coffees

Cacti

Buttercups

Proteas

Mistletoes

GYMNOSPERMS

Pines

Cycads

Gnetales

Ginkgos

BRYOPHYTES

Mosses

Green algae

Hornworts

Liverworts

The Tree of Life

The tree of life is well named, as it looks like the spreading branches of a tree or woody plant. It shows in a simple form how plants have evolved, with the most recent at the top.

The tree of life gives some small idea of the enormous range and diversity of plant life. The earliest plants appeared on Earth around 3.8 billion years ago. These were the algae. Algae are simple plants with no leaves or roots; many can survive only in aquatic environments. More complex plants—the bryophytes, which include mosses, liverworts, and hornworts—started to evolve and colonize the land from around 470 million years ago.

Ferns were the earliest plants to gain height. They were able to do so through the addition of a chemical called lignin in their cell walls. This enabled them to grow taller and straighter than the bryophytes, and as they evolved, they also developed tubes for transporting water and minerals around the plant. Both bryophytes and ferns reproduced by single-cell reproductive structures, called spores.

The first seed plants, which appeared in the fossil record around 350 million years ago, held their seeds in cones—these plants are called gymnosperms. They were followed around 140 million years ago by angiosperms—plants whose seeds develop within a fruit when flowers are successfully fertilized. Seeds have several advantages over spores, including better protection and bigger stores of nutrients, which give the germinating plant an important head start.

Flowering plants then diverged into two major branches known as the monocots (including orchids, palms, and grasses) and eudicots (including buttercups, oaks, and sunflowers). From here came the huge and fascinating variety of plant life we know today: from the tiny to the towering and from beautiful flowers to blooms that look like bees or smell like rotting flesh.

The journey goes on. Not only are scientists continuing to discover new plant species every year (almost every day), but plants are also continuing to evolve in response to changing conditions and new challenges. The story has just begun.

The First Plants

Algae

Earth was formed around 4.6 billion years ago. Fossil evidence indicates the presence of algae, the first plants on Earth, about 3.8 billion years ago. Algae range in size from single cells to giant seaweeds. But they all use sunlight and carbon dioxide from the air to make food (a process called photosynthesis), and they all lack roots, stems, and leaves, as well as a layer of cells surrounding their reproductive cells.

Algae are most commonly found in water, with different species adapted to live in freshwater and saltwater environments. Some species live on land, often in inaccessible locations like rocky crevasses in the highest mountains or buried in the soils of the deepest valleys. This tendency to live in out-of-the-way places and their often very small size make it difficult to count how many different types of algae there are on the planet. Estimates vary widely—from 36,000 to 10 million species. Algae are split into twelve groups called phyla. The three most successful and abundant alga phyla are red algae, green algae, and diatoms.

Key to plate

1: Amphitetras antediluviana
Width: 0.125 millimeters
This is a marine microalga called a diatom. Diatoms are often tiny and usually single-celled. They are important because they are efficient and prolific photosynthesizers and play an important role in regulating the amount of carbon dioxide in the air.

2: Fossil segment of red algae
Bangiomorpha pubescens
Length: 0.225 millimeters
This fossil filament was found in sediments from Arctic Canada and has been dated to around 1.2 billion years ago. It shows characteristic disk-shaped cells surrounded by a sheath, which are features also seen in the filaments of modern-day red algae.

3: Fossil segment of green algae
Cladophora sp.
Length: 0.075 millimeters
Cladophoras are one of the earliest recognizable green algae in the fossil record and are very similar in shape to their modern counterparts. They have been found in fossil deposits dating to around 800 million years ago. These green algae were the precursors to all land plants.

4: Lyrella hennedyi var. neapolitana
Length: 0.06 millimeters
This marine diatom is called Lyrella because it looks a bit like a musical instrument called a lyre.

5: Rhaphoneis amphiceros
Length: 0.06 millimeters
This alga is often found attached to sand grains in shallow marine waters.

6: Acetabularia acetabulum
Height: $^3/_{16}$–4 inches/0.5–10 centimeters
This green alga is found in subtropical marine waters, and although it is a single-celled organism, it is relatively large and has a complicated structure. It has a lower section resembling roots that anchors the plant to rocks, and a long stalk with umbrella-like structures at the end.

7: Red seaweed
Bangia sp.
Height: $2^1/_2$ inches/6 centimeters
The earliest red alga in the fossil record is similar to modern-day red seaweed, in the algae family Bangiophyceae. This marine algae has long red filaments.

8: Pediastrum simplex
Width: 0.06 millimeters
This green alga's cells are arranged in a distinctive genetically determined shape, known as a coenobial colony. It resembles a flattened star.

9: Licmophora flabellata
Height: 0.5 millimeters
Found in shallow marine environments such as estuaries, this diatom has distinctive fans and branching stalks. A sticky substance, secreted from the base of the main stalk, enables it to attach itself to rocks.

10: Asterolampra decora
Width: 0.08 millimeters
A saucer-shaped marine diatom most commonly found in tropical waters.

11: Micrasterias rotata
Width: 0.18 millimeters
This single-celled, freshwater green alga is often found in acidic peatland environments.

12: Asterolampra vulgaris
Width: 0.08 millimeters
Another diatom in the genus Asterolampra (see number 10).

Bryophytes

Plants started to appear on land around 470 million years ago. These earliest land plants evolved from green algae and were similar to present-day liverworts, hornworts, and mosses, which are collectively known as bryophytes. Bryophytes have none of the firm tissue called vascular tissue that enabled later plants to stand upright. This makes bryophytes soft to the touch and unable to grow beyond about 20 inches/50 centimeters in height. They have root-like structures called rhizoids that allow them to capture nutrients from the soil, and a rather unusual reproductive cycle that involves alternating between two different life-forms: a leafy, vegetative form called a gametophyte and a form that disperses spores called a sporophyte. Gametophytes grow most commonly in moist, damp environments. In this form, the plant has male and female organs, which sometimes grow on the same plant and sometimes on separate plants. The female organs are called archegonia and are bottle-shaped. The male organs are called antheridia and are oval. Spermatozoids are released from the male organs to fertilize the egg cells in the bottle-shaped female organs. Once fertilized, the egg is called a zygote and develops into the plant's sporophyte form. The sporophyte produces spores, which ripen and are then released into the air and soil. They grow into gametophytes, and the process starts all over again.

1: Smooth hornwort
Phaeoceros laevis
Height: 2 inches/5 centimeters

2: Yellow moose-dung moss
Splachnum luteum
Height: sporophyte 6 inches/
15 centimeters
The sporophyte has a bright-yellow
parasol-like structure. Insects, rather
than wind, disperse the spores.

3: Reproductive cycle of moss
(a) Male antheridium releasing
spermatozoids (b) Female archegonium
containing egg (c) Fertilized eggs, or
zygote (d) The mature sporophyte

capsule at the top of the moss plant
(e) Spores being released

4: Moss capsules
Height: 2–4 millimeters
(a) *Climacium dendroides* (b) *Tetraphis
pellucida* (c) *Sphagnum palustre*
(d) *Plagiomnium cuspidatum*
These are the spore-bearing capsules,
which have special hoods to protect
the spores inside.

5: Crescent-cup liverwort
Lunularia cruciata
Width: thallus (plant body) $^{1}/_{2}$ inch/
12 millimeters

6: Stiff apple moss
Bartramia ithyphylla
Height: up to $1^{1}/_{2}$ inches/4 centimeters

7: Umbrella liverwort
Marchantia polymorpha
Length: thallus (plant body) $1^{1}/_{2}$–$2^{1}/_{2}$
inches/4–6 centimeters; female
receptacles 20–45 millimeters

8: *Asterella australis*
Length: thallus (plant body) $1^{1}/_{2}$ inches/
4 centimeters

Fungi and Lichens

Two groups of organisms—fungi and lichens—were vital in helping plants gain a foothold on dry land around 470 to 400 million years ago. Do note that although this is a book about plants, neither fungi or lichen are plants. Fungi don't make food by photosynthesis and they don't have roots. They are included here because they were historically treated as plants and because they are involved in the functioning of plant ecosystems. Fungi help to break down plant litter and animal remains in soil, ensuring that there are sufficient nutrients for plants to take up for growth. Fungi are also an important food source for animals and humans. For example, yeast is a fungus and is an essential ingredient in bread and beer. At the same time, fungi are also responsible for some of the most toxic poisons and most dangerous diseases of both humans and animals. Many fungi are highly poisonous and should never be touched or eaten when found growing in the wild.

Lichens are a collaboration between a fungal element and photosynthesizing algae. The organic acid released from rock-inhabiting lichens is thought to have been important for breaking down rocks to make soil in the earliest land environments. Lichens are also able to survive in harsh places with extreme climates, an ability that would have been essential for early life on land. Species of lichen are found on rocks growing at the top of the highest mountains and in the hottest and coldest deserts. Some even produce their own sunscreen in the form of sun-protecting pigments. Production of the pigments is triggered by high levels of sunlight; it enables these lichens to grow in open environments with little or no shade.

Key to plate

1: Bird's nest fungus
Cyathus striatus
Diameter: $^3/_8$ inch/1 centimeter
These tiny fungi hold their spores in disk-shaped packets resembling eggs in a nest. Raindrops cause the spores to spring out and disperse.

2: Red *Marasmius*
Marasmius haematocephalus
Height: $^3/_4$–$1^1/_4$ inches/2–3 centimeters
These small, umbrella-like fungi play an important role in recycling the litter layer on forest floors.

3: Pixie-cup lichen
Cladonia chlorophaea
Height: $^3/_8$–$1^1/_2$ inches/1–4 centimeters
These lichens form stalked cups—from which, according to European folklore, pixies sip morning dew.

4: Leathery goblet
Cymatoderma elegans
Height: 6 inches/15 centimeters
The cap of this fungus opens to a wide funnel and can often be found containing water, hence its name.

5: Veiled lady
Phallus indusiatus
Height: 10 inches/25 centimeters
This distinctive fungus has been used for centuries in traditional medicine.

6: Enokitake mushroom
Flammulina velutipes (cultivated form)
Height: 4 inches/10 centimeters
Commonly used in East Asian cooking, this mushroom is cultivated in a carbon dioxide–rich environment to encourage long, thin stems.

7: Turkey-tail fungus
Trametes versicolor
Diameter: $1^1/_2$–4 inches/4–10 centimeters
This fungus is named because its radiating growth resembles the fanned tails of turkeys.

8: Golden shield lichen
Xanthoria parietina
Diameter: up to 4 inches/10 centimeters
This lichen is bright yellow-orange in sunny places but a dull green when in the shade because it makes its own sunscreen in the form of a sun-protecting pigment.

9: Fly agaric
Amanita muscaria
Diameter: 3–8 inches/8–20 centimeters
This toadstool often appears in fairy tales. Its toxic chemicals can cause hallucinations.

10: Lane Cove waxcap
Hygrocybe lanecovensis
Height: up to 2 inches/5 centimeters
An endangered fungus, first collected in 1998 and known from a single parkland in Sydney, Australia.

Club Mosses, Horsetails, and Whisk Ferns

The common names we use for plants are sometimes not an accurate reflection of scientific definitions. Club mosses, for example, are not actually mosses but, rather, vascular plants. This means that they contain a well-developed system of specialized cells known as vascular bundles, which allow the plants to grow upright and much taller than bryophytes, which lack a vascular system (see pages 10–11). Horsetails and whisk ferns also contain vascular strands.

These three groups of plants, which reproduce by spores, have ancient lineages and are often referred to as living fossils, because there are fossil remains dating from 400 to 370 million years ago that are very similar in structure to the club mosses, horsetails, and whisk ferns we see growing today. There's one important difference, though: the present-day plants are small herbs, usually less than 3 feet/1 meter tall. By comparison, their ancestors were giants. Horsetail and lycophyte trees (related to club mosses), towering up to 130 feet/40 meters, dominated the early Carboniferous landscapes (see pages 18–19). The giant tree forms of these plants met the fate of most species of life on Earth—extinction—when they were outcompeted by better adapted rivals, leaving only the miniature forms that were able to survive.

Key to plate

1: **Club moss**
Selaginella lepidophylla
Height: 4 inches/10 centimeters
Club mosses have small, scale-like leaves wrapped all around their stems.

2: **Whisk fern**
Psilotum complanatum
Height: up to 30 inches/75 centimeters
This species of whisk fern is usually found hanging from the trunks of trees in tropical regions. It does not have roots or leaves but has small scales on the stem.

3: **Horsetail**
Equisetum hyemale
Height: ³/₈ inch/1 centimeter
Cone
The spores of horsetails come from sporangia, which are produced at the margin of polygonal structures grouped into a cone. Cones are usually situated at the apex (top) of the plant.

4: **Field horsetail**
Equisetum arvense
Diameter: 3–5 millimeters
Cross section through stem
This cross section through a young horsetail stem shows the vascular bundles (the seed-shaped sections) that extend up through the whole stem, enabling the upward movement of water and sap.

5: **Field horsetail**
Equisetum arvense
The vegetative shoots of field horsetails have whorled branches and look feathery. The actual leaves are small, papery, and fused into a sheath on the stem. The cones that contain the spores are found on pale, fertile shoots, which grow before the bigger green vegetative ones. Field horsetails grow in damp or wet places.

6: **Sporophyll of a club moss**
Lycopodium clavatum
Length: 2–2.5 millimeters
Sporophylls are tiny leaves that bear spore-production structures called sporangia.

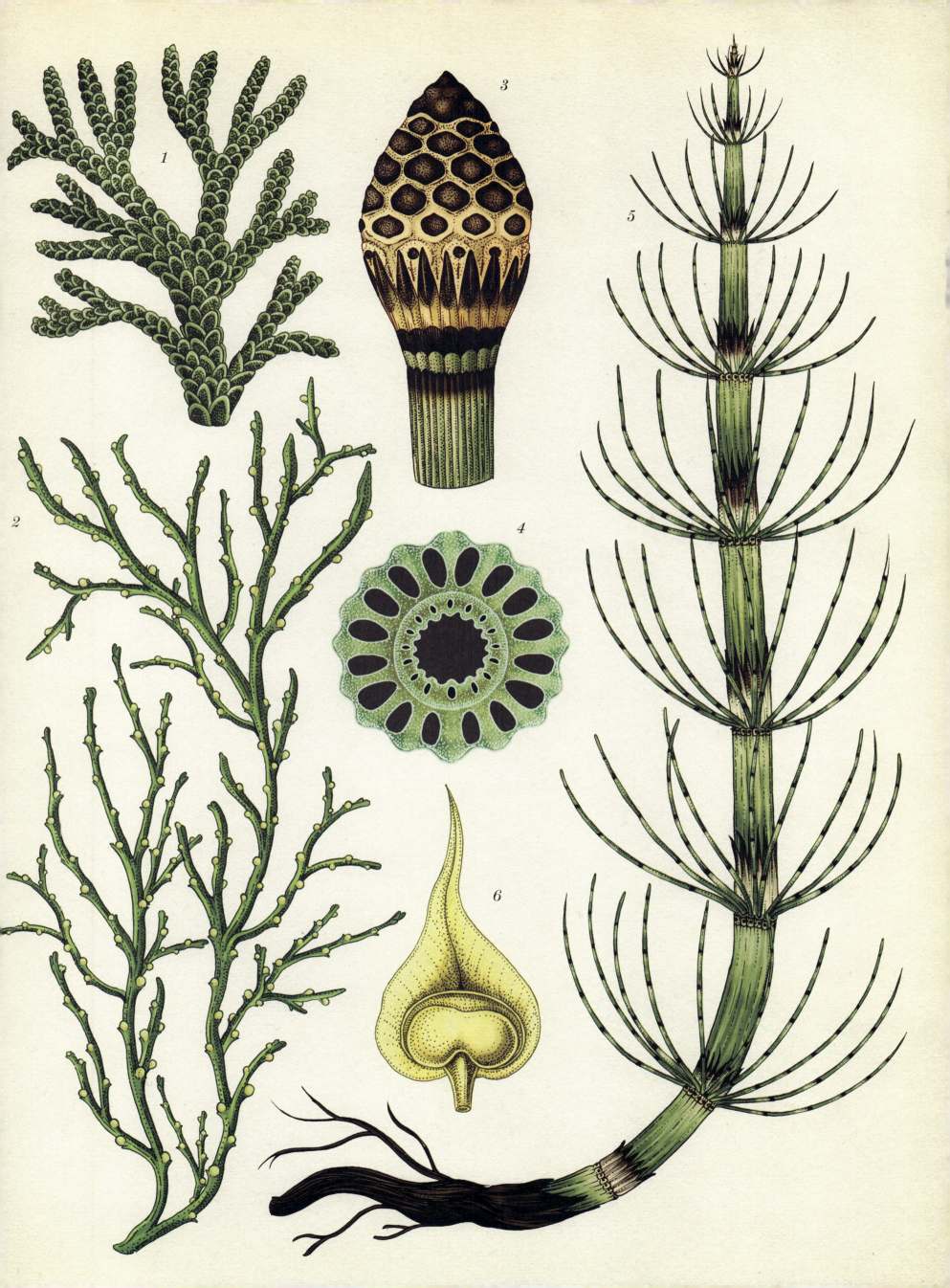

Ferns

Ferns are found in a huge variety of environments across the globe. Mostly they prefer moist, shady environments, but there are species found in deserts, underwater, and floating on top of ponds and rivers. They take many different forms, from upright plants with roots that grow in the soil to epiphytic plants, which grow on other plants (usually trees) with their roots waving freely in the air and gaining moisture and nutrients from rain and debris. Some ferns also grow as vines. All ferns are herbaceous, which means that none contain the woody material that forms the central parts of tree trunks (known as the secondary xylem). Despite this, some fern species do still grow to the height of trees. These ferns have a stem containing a central core filled with pith surrounded by strands of vascular tissue. This forms a rigid cylinder, or trunk, and a structure that can move water, sugars, and nutrients around the plant. These tree-form ferns dominated the Carboniferous forests of 350 million years ago (see pages 18–19) and could reach as high as 33 feet/10 meters. Tree ferns are still with us today.

Another distinctive characteristic of ferns is a reproductive cycle that involves two different forms of the same plant alternating between generations. Ripe spores are released from the underside of the leaves. These grow into small plants, called gametophytes (also part of bryophyte reproduction; see pages 10–11), which look quite unlike their ferny parent. Usually, the gametophyte is a tiny, flat, green, scale-like growth, just a few centimeters long and rarely seen. When this plant matures, it produces male and female organs. These then produce offspring, which grow into the same ferny form as their grandparents, the plant we would readily recognize as a fern, known as a sporophyte. This form then produces spores on the underside of its leaves, and the cycle continues.

Key to plate

1: **East Indian holly fern**
Arachniodes aristata
Pinnule (leaflet) length: $^1/_2$ inch/
1.5 centimeters
The underside of a leafy pinnule showing the disk-like structures called sori, in which the spores are produced. The sori are protected by a white membrane called indusium.

2: **Stag's horn fern**
Platycerium superbum
Length of fronds: up to $6^1/_2$ feet/
2 meters
This species develops round, thick fronds at its base, which protect the roots and collect detritus to create a soil for the epiphytic plant, and thinner foliage fronds, which bear the spores.

3: **Maidenhair fern**
Adiantum capillus-veneris
Height: up to 1 foot/30 centimeters
Stem with fronds
This plant can hang from vertical surfaces or grow upright from horizontal ones.

4: **Polypodium verrucosum**
Length of fronds: up to 3 feet/1 meter
Fronds
This plant's fronds have rows of wart-like bumps on their upper surface that hold spores.

5: **Silver tree fern**
Cyathea dealbata
Height: up to 33 feet/10 meters
Unfurling frond
This is one of the large tree ferns of the tropics and subtropics. The fronds have characteristic silvery undersides. Almost all ferns have their fronds tightly coiled into a spiral called a fern crozier before they unfurl.

6: **Deer fern**
Blechnum spicant
Fertile frond length: up to 28 inches/
70 centimeters

This fern has two types of fronds: sterile fronds, which are evergreen, and seasonal, fertile fronds, which are usually grouped in the plant's center.

7: **Sporangium**
Diameter: less than 1 millimeter
Sporangia are spore vessels found on all ferns; they are grouped into clusters called sori and produce large numbers of spores. Sporangia are pale first and darken as the spores mature. When the spores are well developed, and if the external conditions are suitable, the sporangia rip wide apart and release the spores.

8: **Cross section through leaf bearing sporangia**
Section diameter: 3 millimeters
The sporangia, where spores are produced, radiate out from a receptacle around the vein. The vein appears darker on the illustration.

Environment: Carboniferous Forests

The transition from the first, small, herbaceous land plants to massive trees 130 to 165 feet/40 to 50 meters high occurred over 90 million years, between 389 and 299 million years ago. By the end of this period, known as the Carboniferous period, the Earth was covered with dense forests of thick-trunked trees, up to 3 feet/1 meter in diameter. Many of the trees appear to have been giant versions of the herbaceous plants from which they evolved. They included huge lycophyte trees (related to club mosses), giant horsetails, and very large tree ferns. None of them had flowers, and many still reproduced by spores. But these earliest forests also gave us the first trees that reproduced by seeds. The seeds were produced in simple cones, very like the ones seen on conifer trees today.

The Earth of 350 million years ago looked very different from today. The landmasses that later formed our continents were all in different places. South Africa and South America were at the South Pole, and most of the continental plates that now form Europe, China, and Australia were at the Equator. Forests responded to the climates associated with their locations. The tropical belt—warm, wet, and seasonal—was covered in swamp forests of lycophytes and seed ferns, which relished the sweaty humidity and pools of standing water. When these trees died, they fell over, became waterlogged, and sank. Over millions of years, they became compacted and fossilized into coal. In drier forests, outside the tropical belt, giant horsetails and early seed ferns dominated alongside lycophyte trees that were much shorter than their tropical cousins. Scientists think their smaller size was an adaptation to make them more resistant to drought.

Key to plate

1: Gilboa trees
Eospermatopteris
Height: 26 feet/8 meters
The Gilboa is the earliest known tree, dating to 385 million years ago, based on fossil deposits found in western New York. Its trunk had a crown of leafless branches at the top. The plant probably photosynthesized through its trunk. Some of the tree's branches contained sporangia at their ends, and these contained the spores. The tree achieved great height by having long roots to anchor it to the ground.

2: Cordaites tree
Height: up to 98 feet/30 meters
Cordaites trees occupied a large range of habitats from mangroves to drier uplands. Their most important feature was the fact that they reproduced by seeds and had cones similar in structure to a present-day conifer tree.

3: *Lepidodendron* trees
Height: up to 115 feet/35 meters
This tree had a dense crown of simple leaves that grew directly from the stem, with no leaf stalk. This type of leaf attachment resulted in a triangular shape on the stem when the leaf fell off, resulting in a beautifully patterned trunk.

4: Tree fern
Psaronius
Height: up to 33 feet/10 meters
Fossil remains of this tree are often found in coal deposits because it grew in Carboniferous swamps. It was one of the largest tree ferns to grow during this time. It had large fronds for leaves, similar to those of ferns.

5: Seed-fern tree
Medullosa noei
Height: up to 33 feet/10 meters
This tree had fern-like leaves, spirally arranged around the stem, but it reproduced by seeds. The seeds looked very similar to present-day cycad seeds, suggesting a close evolutionary relationship.

6: *Archaeopteris* tree
Height: 30 feet/9 meters
This was a major tree in Devonian and Carboniferous landscapes. It is thought to be an ancestor of all seed plants because it had stems with wood similar to that found in conifers; however, it still reproduced by spores.

Trees

Conifers

Conifers make up around 30 percent of the world's forests and can survive in some of the coldest and most hostile places on Earth. Most of them are easily identified by their simple, needle-like leaves and distinctive cones. Many are evergreen and don't lose their leaves in winter. Less immediately obvious is that conifers don't have flowers. Instead, they have simpler organs for making seeds, called cones.

All conifer trees have two kinds of cones: male and female. Some species have both kinds on the same tree, while others have separate male and female trees. Male cones are usually small and produce multiple grains of yellow pollen. The female cone is made up of woody interlocking scales. Once fertilized by pollen released from the male cone, it starts to grow, sometimes to a very large size (like the *Araucaria* cone, for example, which is the size of a soccer ball). This process takes from a few months to a year. During the process, the female cone remains green and tightly closed, with gluey resin keeping it shut. When mature, the cone turns brown, the scales separate, and seeds are released to be dispersed by wind or animals.

Conifers use a number of external triggers to determine when to release the mature seeds: temperature, or sometimes fire, can indicate to the plant that the ground around it has been cleared, creating plenty of space for its seed to grow.

Key to plate

1: Chinese golden larch
Pseudolarix amabilis
Height: 130–165 feet/40–50 meters
Seed cone and shoot
This deciduous conifer loses its needles during cold and dry weather. It has male and female reproductive organs on the same plant. Male pollen stalks are around 3/8–3/4 inch/1–2 centimeters and female cones around 1 1/2–2 3/4 inches/4–7 centimeters long.

2: Bald cypress
Taxodium distichum
Height: 130–150 feet/40–45 meters
Female cone
This tree is dominant in river floodplains and swamps in the southeastern United States.

3: Hinoki cypress
Chamaecyparis obtusa
Height: 130–165 feet/40–50 meters
Female cone
This tree has small eight-scaled cones. Wood from this tree has been used for centuries in its native Japan for the construction of traditional buildings.

4: Korean fir
Abies koreana
Height: 33–60 feet/10–18 meters
Female cone and leaves

Native to the mountains of Korea, this tree has dark-green needle-like leaves and blue or purple cones.

5: Scots pine
Pinus sylvestris
Pollen grain diameter: 0.06 millimeters
(a) Pollen grain (b) Male cone
Conifer pollen often has distinctive air-bladders that allow it to be carried on the wind, creating great yellow 'clouds' over the forest. This method of dispersal allows the pollen to travel huge distances by air or water. Pine pollen has been found trapped in the ice at the North Pole, many thousands of miles from the nearest tree.

6: Chilean podocarp
Podocarpus nubigenus
Height: 115 feet/35 meters
Leaves and seeds
This tree grows in the temperate rain forest of southern Chile. It develops only one seed, with a juicy, swollen stalk, which makes it look and taste like a fruit. This attracts birds for dispersal.

7: European silver fir
Abies alba
Height: 200 feet/60 meters
(a) Seed scales (b) Bract, which are modified leaves

8: Monkey puzzle tree
Araucaria araucana
Height: 165 feet/50 meters
Shoot with leaves and male cones
This tree is native to southwest Argentina and southern and central Chile. It was given its name by an observer who thought that monkeys wouldn't be able to climb its spiky branches.

9: Cedar of Lebanon
Cedrus libani
Height: up to 130 feet/40 meters
Female cone
Lebanon's flag includes the image of this cedar, which is named after Mount Lebanon, where it can be found. The largest populations, however, are in the Taurus Mountains of southern Turkey. The tree produces large cones, 3–5 inches/8–12 centimeters long.

10: Loblolly pine
Pinus taeda
Height: 82–108 feet/25–33 meters
Female cone, branch, and leaves
This is the most important and widely cultivated timber species in the southern United States.

The Giant Sequoia

Giant sequoias are record breakers. They are the tallest trees on the planet, some growing to over 260 feet/80 meters. Their trunks can be up to 36 feet/11 meters wide, meaning it takes sixteen adults holding hands to reach around one. They live for a long time, with many individual trees surviving for more than two thousand years. Fossil records indicate that sequoias have been around for a large part of Earth's history — 100 million years. These giants are genuine living fossils.

Sequoias are conifers. Like all conifers, they reproduce with cones. Male and female cones are carried on the same tree. These cones are small (especially compared to the size of the tree!) and grow at the ends of branches. Sequoias are well adapted to their environment. Bark as thick as 24 inches/60 centimeters and foliage high above the ground provide protection from fire.

The trees' great height requires physical adaptations. Sequoia roots spread out for up to 98 feet/30 meters beyond the tree, intertwining with other tree roots to provide anchorage for the huge trunk, but not penetrating very deep into the ground. The speed

at which this tree grows when young is nothing short of phenomenal. In Italy, a young tree reached a height of 72 feet/22 meters in just seventeen years.

Key to plate

Giant sequoia
Sequoiadendron giganteum
1: **Tree**
Height: up to 265 feet/80 meters
This tree is native to California and is found on the western slopes of the Sierra Nevada, where it occurs in about seventy-five distinct groves.

2: **Female cone**
Length: 2–2³/₄ inches/5–7 centimeters
Because sequoia cones grow high up the tree, they are difficult to count, but one tree is thought to produce as many as 11,000 cones a year.

3: **Leaves**
As well as enabling the tree to photosynthesize, sequoia leaves have an important role in water retention. Sequoias have no leaves on the lower part of the trunk, only high up where the leaves can absorb and retain atmospheric moisture. The leaf surface absorbs water like a sponge, storing it for use by the uppermost part of the tree.

4: **Wood and bark**
Sequoia wood and bark are surprisingly soft and light, making them flexible and less likely to collapse under their own weight or in high winds. They move large volumes of water around their huge frames each day, causing the trunk to swell and contract during each daily cycle.

The Ginkgo

Ginkgos are beautiful trees. They grace the parks and streets of cities all over the world, partly because of their looks but also because they are fairly resistant to the extremes of weather and to the pollution found in cities. In the wild, ginkgos occur naturally in some parts of China.

Wild or cultivated, the ginkgos we see today belong to only one species, *Ginkgo biloba*. This tree represents the end of an evolutionary line. Around 250 million years ago, there were numerous different types of ginkgos growing all over the world. All have now died out, apart from *Ginkgo biloba*. *Ginkgo biloba* seems not to have changed its appearance that much in those 250 million years. The modern leaf appears to be identical in shape and form to examples found in the fossil record, and ginkgos are often called living fossils.

The leaves of ginkgos look like fans, both in shape and in the pattern of parallel veins on their underside. Ginkgos are deciduous, losing their leaves when the weather becomes cold. They grow to 98–108 feet/30–40 meters in height. Like conifers, they evolved before flowering plants and are gymnosperms, with male and female reproductive structures on their stalks instead of flowers. Male and female *Ginkgo biloba* trees are different and separate. Female trees have ovules, or seeds, that grow from the base of the leaf axis on stalks called peduncles, with one seed on each stalk.

Key to plate

Ginkgo tree
Ginkgo biloba
1: **Leaves and ovules on branch of female tree**
Height: 130 feet/40 meters
Ginkgo biloba can be very long lived; the oldest recorded individual is thought to be 3,500 years old. What appear to be

plum-like fruits are actually naked seeds. Although they may look appetizing, they emit a terrible stench like vomit. Ginkgo seeds were probably adapted to be dispersed by carrion-eating dinosaurs, which would explain the unsavory smell.

2: **Catkins from male tree**
Male trees have catkin-like structures, which grow in pairs at the base of the leaf axis and bear distinctive pollen grains. These are wind dispersed.

1   2

Temperate Trees

Temperate trees are found in mid-latitude parts of the globe, between the polar regions and the tropics. In these regions, summers are warm and wet and winters cold and dry. The trees that grow here have to be able to withstand different kinds of climate and periods of rapid change.

One of the most significant seasonal changes in temperate regions is the number of hours of sunlight. There is less sunlight in autumn and winter, and therefore less opportunity for trees to photosynthesize. Many temperate trees react by shedding their leaves. These are known as deciduous trees, and the process is called leaf abscission. Trees will also shed their leaves if conditions become unusually dry, because most water loss from a plant is through its leaves. Shedding its leaves saves the tree water. It also accounts for the colors of temperate woodlands in autumn. Because the leaves are no longer required to photosynthesize, they lose their chlorophyll, the green pigment used for photosynthesis. This means that other colors in the leaf become apparent, producing the glorious displays of reds, browns, and golds seen in the forests of New England, northern Japan, and other temperate regions.

Shedding leaves has another advantage. Most temperate trees have large, flat leaves (very different from the needle-like leaves of conifers), which are attached to the branches by a small stem called a petiole. The leaves' shape makes them excellent for capturing energy when the sun is shining, but it also makes the tree vulnerable to damage when it snows, because the leaves tend to trap the snow, making the branch heavy and likely to break.

Temperate trees shed their leaves by growing a layer of cells between the leaf stalk and the branch, which separates stalk from branch and causes the leaf to fall to the ground. A hormone called auxin controls this process. The vast majority of temperate trees (including all those on this page) are angiosperms, or flowering plants, that evolved late—between 150 and 80 million years ago, almost 150 million years later than the conifers.

Key to plate

1: **Sycamore**
Acer pseudoplatanus
Height: up to 115 feet/35 meters
(a) Bud (b) Seed
This tree is native to the mountains of central Europe and has been introduced elsewhere.

2: **White mulberry tree**
Morus alba
Height: over 66 feet/20 meters
(a) Leaves (b) Fruit
This species is native to China and is the main food source for silkworms.

3: **English oak**
Quercus robur
Height: 118 feet/36 meters
(a) Leaf (b) Acorn
These trees occur almost all over Europe.

4: **English elm**
Ulmus procera
Height: 118 feet/36 meters
(a) Seed (b) Flower

5: **Common beech**
Fagus sylvatica
Height: 130 feet/40 meters
(a) Seedpod (b) Leaf

6: **Sweet chestnut**
Castanea sativa
Height: 115 feet/35 meters
(a) Leaf (b) Seed

7: **Scarlet oak**
Quercus coccinea
Height: 69 feet/21 meters
(a) Leaf (b) Acorns

8: **Silver birch**
Betula pendula
Height: 98 feet/30 meters
(a) Male catkin (b) Scale from female catkin (c) Female flower (d) Male flower

9: **Oregon maple**
Acer macrophyllum
Height: 49–98 feet/15–30 meters
Leaf

10: **Japanese maple**
Acer palmatum
Height: 26 feet/8 meters
Leaf

Tropical Trees

The tropics, the regions to the near north and south of the Equator, are warm, with temperatures averaging 68–77°F/20–25°C, and with daylight hours the same all year round. Some parts also experience large amounts of rainfall, providing very wet environments. Whereas trees in temperate regions, whose growth is affected by winter cold and darkness, exhibit growth rings in their trunks, trees in tropical regions, whose growth is steady through the year, do not. The bark of tropical trees tends to be smooth, pale, and thin—often less than 4 inches/10 millimeters in thickness.

Trees in the tropics come in many different shapes and sizes. Their forms are largely determined by local variations in temperature and rainfall. In areas with long dry seasons, such as the Caatinga region of Brazil, trees rarely grow taller than 33 feet/10 meters and tend to be deciduous, losing their leaves during the dry season. These trees also have very deep roots to cope with the intervals of drought. In the wettest parts of the tropics, such as the Amazon rain forest, trees are tall (often 98 feet/30 meters or more), evergreen (because they can photosynthesize efficiently all year round), and have little protection against cold or drought (because they don't need it).

In order to stay upright, the tallest tropical trees need good anchorage, so they have evolved a spectacular kind of aboveground rooting system called buttresses (like flying buttresses on a Gothic cathedral) that spread out from the main trunk, often leaving gaps big enough for humans to walk through. Other tropical trees have thinner, stilt-like roots that sprout higher up the trunk. In the wettest parts of the tropics, many leaves have what is called a drip tip, which allows water to drain quickly from the leaf's surface. Leaves are usually elliptical, thick, and large—up to 5 inches/13 centimeters long.

Key to plate

1: Cannonball tree
Couroupita guianensis
Height: 75 feet/23 meters
Flowers and buds on stem
Native to the Guianas in South America, this tree has complex, waxy flowers that are beautifully scented and grow directly on the bark of the trunk. Its fruits look like rusty cannonballs hanging in clusters.

2: Rubber tree
Hevea brasiliensis
Height: up to 130 feet/40 meters
(a) Leaves (b) Seedpod
Native to parts of Brazil and the Guianas region of northeastern South America. The milky latex of *Hevea brasiliensis* is the raw material for natural rubber. Each fruit of the rubber tree contains three seeds.

3: Ackee
Blighia sapida
Height: up to 98 feet/30 meters
(a) Cross section through fruit
(b) Fruit and leaves on stem
Although this tree is native to West Africa, it is widespread in Jamaica and featured in Jamaica's national dish, ackee and saltfish. The brightly colored fruits contain three large black seeds, each with a yellowish-white appendage called an aril. This aril, which has the texture of scrambled egg, is the only edible part of this poisonous fruit, and even this becomes edible only after the fruit is fully ripe. Eating it before then can result in what is known as Jamaican vomiting sickness.

4: Indian banyan tree
Ficus benghalensis
Height: up to 98 feet/30 meters
Leaves on stem
Native to India and Pakistan, the banyan is a type of strangling fig. It begins life growing on other trees and eventually envelops them completely, its aerial roots becoming trunks. It has leathery leaves and bright-orange fruit.

1

2a

2b

3a

3b

4

Fruit Trees

Humans have always eaten fruit: archaeologists have found 4,500-year-old banana remains in human settlements in Africa, and the United Kingdom has many Bronze Age sites containing four-thousand-year-old cherrystones. This long history speaks to fruit's practicality as a food source, since most varieties can be eaten straight off the tree.

But why do plants produce fruits? The answer is reproduction. All fruits carry the plant's seed. Many fruits, such as apples and pears, contain their seeds at the center of their fleshy pulp. Some, such as cherries and peaches, have one large seed in the form of a stone. Some fruits, such as blackberries and strawberries, carry their seeds attached to their outsides. And some citrus and tropical fruits, including bananas and oranges, whose hot environments could dry out exposed pulp, have a firm skin enclosing both their flesh and seeds.

The flesh of a fruit is tasty and nutritious. There are good evolutionary reasons for this. Many plants rely on animals and birds to disperse their seed. By enclosing them in juicy fruit, the plant gets its seed nibbled by peckish passersby, who then pass it through their digestive systems and deposit it, suitably fertilized, in a fresh growing environment some distance away.

But fruit isn't just what's in your fruit bowl or your fruit salad. Coffee comes from a fruit, and so does cacao, from which chocolate is made. These two delicacies have been important international commodities for hundreds of years.

Key to plate

1: **Cacao**
Theobroma cacao
Height: 26 feet/8 meters
(a) Cross section through fruit
(b) Flower
The fruit of cacao is a thick-walled pod that contains lots of large seeds embedded in sweet-tasting pulp. The fermented and dried seeds are ground up to yield cocoa powder, which is used to make chocolate. The edible properties of *cacao* were discovered more than two thousand years ago by the people of Central America.

2: **Coffee**
Coffea arabica
Height: 26 feet/8 meters
(a) Cross section through fruit
(b) Flower (c) Leaves and fruits
Coffee is one of the world's favorite drinks, one of the most important commercial crop plants, and the second most valuable international commodity. *Coffea Arabica*, said to produce the finest coffee beans, is native to northeast Africa. Coffee trees' small red fruits, called drupes, contain two stones, or beans, each enclosing a single seed.

3: **Cashew**
Anacardium occidentale
Height: 46 feet/14 meters
Leaves and fruits
This tropical evergreen tree originally came from northeastern Brazil. The fruit of the cashew nut looks like a pear with a hard kidney-shaped attachment. The pear-shaped fleshy part, called the cashew apple, is in fact the swollen stalk of the fruit. The hard kidney-shaped part of the fruit contains the seed, which we call a cashew nut.

4: **Banana**
Musa acuminata
Height: 49 feet/15 meters
Flower
Musa acuminata is the wild ancestor of the cultivated banana. Thousands of years of domestication have produced a delicious edible fruit. The yellow variety known as the Cavendish, found in many supermarkets, represents just a small proportion of global production.

5: **Peach**
Prunus persica
Height: up to 33 feet/10 meters

Cut open fruit with leaf
Peaches are drupes, each fruit containing a stone with one seed.

6: **Durian**
Durio zibethinus
Height: up to 98 feet/30 meters
Cut open fruit with flowers
The large, heavy, spiky fruits of the durian tree contain several big seeds wrapped in an edible aril, or seed appendage. When fully ripe, the delicious aril has the texture of thick custard cream. Ripe durians have a notoriously strong smell.

1a   1b   2a   2b

2c

4

3

5

6

Ornamental Shrubs

From the seventeenth century, collecting beautiful plants from all over the world to show in private and public gardens became an important component of European trade. Wealthy individuals competed with one another, paying professional plant hunters to scour the world looking for new discoveries. They built themselves increasingly elaborate hothouses and glasshouses to show off their finds, which included everything from delicate orchids (see pages 72–75) to giant water lilies (see pages 84–85). But there was also a vigorous trade in plants for the garden. In Holland in the 1630s, inflated prices for the coveted Viceroy tulip led to the first recorded financial market collapse. In some regions of the world where plants were collected, environments were depleted of their native species by plant hunters, some to the point of extinction.

Because ornamental trees and shrubs need to grow outside all year round, a key objective for the plant hunter was to find types that can tolerate the cold and damp of northern European winters. For this reason, many ornamental shrubs that are common today come from regions with similar temperatures to parts of Europe. The majority originate from the Himalaya region of China, with Central America and eastern North America the next most common regions.

Key to plate

1: Fuchsia
Fuchsia triphylla
Height: up to 3 feet/1 meter
Leaves and flowers
This small shrub originates from Haiti and the Dominican Republic and is one of more than 110 species of fuchsias found in gardens the world over. It has very attractive flowers, which bloom from early spring to late autumn.

2: Southern magnolia
Magnolia grandifolia
Height: up to 82 feet/25 meters
Vertical cross section through flower
This large evergreen magnolia tree,

native to the southeastern United States, has large, fragrant white flowers. The tree's timber is often used to make furniture.

3: King protea or Cape artichoke
Protea cynaroides
Height: up to 6½ feet/2 meters
Flower
This is a sparsely branched evergreen shrub with leathery leaves and large bowl-shaped flower heads. The flower heads are covered with pink or cream triangular bracts—which are not in fact petals but modified leaves—enclosing many long flowers massed together in

the center. This is the national flower of South Africa and has a natural distribution in temperate South Africa.

4: Saucer magnolia
Magnolia × soulangeana
Height: up to 20 feet/6 meters
Flowers and buds on branch
This magnolia is a small deciduous shrub with large white, pink, or purple goblet-shaped flowers. It is a popular garden hybrid produced from two natural species from China.

Environment: Rain Forests

Rain forests are rich and fascinating environments. They develop in places where every month is wet (with 4 inches/10 centimeters of rainfall or more) and where there are high temperatures (64°F/18°C or more) all year round. Globally, there are three main blocks of rain forest: in Central and South America, in central Africa, and in Southeast Asia. Permanently wet and warm, rain forests provide such fertile growing environments that many different kinds of plants live alongside (and often underneath) one another there. These plants have different strategies for sharing the abundant natural resources: some are tall and thin, spreading thick canopies high above the ground to catch the sun; others cling on to another plant; and still others creep along the ground in the dark, drawing nutrients from the rich, damp soil.

The tallest rain-forest trees stick high out of the canopy. These are known as emergents and include elegant giants like the Brazil nut tree, which can grow to 165 feet/ 50 meters. Emergent trees typically have slim trunks and produce branches and leaves only at the top.

Beneath the emergents is the canopy layer, often evergreen or semi-evergreen, where plants grow close together in a dense layer of vegetation. When seen from above, a rain-forest canopy can look like rolling, grassy hills.

Below the canopy is the understory, home to plants that can photosynthesize effectively from the limited sunlight that penetrates the canopy. These include vines, creepers, epiphytes (plants that grow on other plants), huge spreading ferns, swamp dwellers such as mangroves, and fungi, which flourish in the organically rich soil.

The number and variety of species in rain forests are staggering. In one area in Ecuador, every other tree was found to be of a different species. In one 200-acre/ 80-hectare area of the Rio Palenque forest, there are 1,030 species. (By contrast, there are 1,380 seed plant species in the whole of the British Isles.)

A rain forest is a dynamic system, constantly changing and regenerating. When a big tree dies, it crashes to the ground, opening up a gap in the canopy. Sunlight streams in, and life begins again. The fallen trunk then becomes a world in itself, providing a habitat for all sorts of plants and animals as it rots.

Gallery 3

Palms and Cycads

Cycads

Palms

The Oil Palm

Cycads

When you first see a cycad you might be forgiven for thinking it was a palm tree. The long, frond-like leaves emerging like a crown from the top of the trunk give these plants a distinctly palm-like appearance. In fact, they are much older than the palm family. They evolved around 318 million years ago, probably from seed ferns. This makes cycads the most ancient lineage of living seed plants.

Unlike palms, cycads do not flower but are gymnosperms, bearing their reproductive organs in cones, as conifers and ginkgos do. Cycads have separate male and female plants; the male plant's cones contain pollen, while the female plant's cones contain ovules that become seeds. Cycads have a long, cylindrical trunk and usually no branches. Leaves grow directly from the top of the trunk and typically fall off as the tree gets older, leaving the trunk with a textured diamond pattern on the stem and a crown of leaves at the top. Today, there are around three hundred species of cycads. They are found in a wide range of environments, from the tropics and subtropics to warm temperate regions. All cycads live for a long time, some for more than one thousand years.

Cycads were long thought to be pollinated by the wind, as conifers are. However, studies now suggest that the vast majority, if not all, are actually pollinated by small beetles called weevils. Cycad seeds are large and have a fleshy outer coat, a tempting treat for a wide range of birds, rodents, and bats. These animals help disperse seeds quickly—a useful trick, as the seeds don't live very long and are vulnerable to drying out.

Key to plate

1: **Eastern Cape giant cycad**
Encephalartos altensteinii
Height: 20 feet/6 meters
The Eastern Cape giant cycad comes from South Africa, is very long-lived and slow growing (as slow as 1 inch/2.5 centimeters per year), and is popular as an ornamental plant. In the wild, it is found near the coast in habitats ranging from open shrubland on steep rocky slopes to closed evergreen forests in valleys.

2: **Encephalartos ferox**
Height: 3 feet/1 meter
Leaf
This species has bright orange-red cones. The very large female cones consist of many densely packed cone scales, each of which bears two large seeds. It occurs in northern KwaZulu-Natal province of South Africa and southern Mozambique at low elevations, between 66 and 330 feet/20 and 100 meters above sea level.

3: **Marlboro blue cycad**
Cycas angulata
Height: 6¹/₂–30 feet/2–9 meters
Maturing seeds on the female plant
Unlike most cycads, female *Cycas* plants produce round seeds rather than condensed, compacted cones. This Australian cycad has distinctive glossy blue-green leaves 3–4¹/₂ feet/100–140 centimeters long.

4: Sago palm
Cycas revoluta
Height: 3–10 feet/1–3 meters
Leaf
This cycad is found in Japan and in China's coastal Fujian Province. Although *Cycas revoluta* is often called the sago palm and is sometimes processed for sago (a powdered food starch), the source of most cultivated sago is the true sago palm, *Metroxylon sagu,* which is an actual palm rather than a cycad.

Palms

Palms are one of the most important flowering plant families in the world. There are more than 2,600 different species. They include many record breakers: the raffia palm, for instance, is the plant with the longest leaves (82 feet/25 meters). The coco de mer palm has the largest seed (up to 12 inches/30 centimeters long and weighing 40 pounds/18 kilograms). And the talipot palm has the largest flower clusters (26 feet/8 meters long, with multiple clusters containing as many as 24 million flowers on a branched stalk). Palms also contribute some of the most valuable crops to the world economy, including coconuts, dates, betel nuts, and palm oil (see pages 44–45).

Palms are found in tropical and subtropical regions throughout the world, with the greatest number of different species occurring in tropical rain forests. Unlike the similar-looking cycads, palms are flowering plants. They evolved relatively recently, around 100 million years ago, and diversified in the earliest tropical rain forests.

Palms are recognizable by their large evergreen leaves that emerge from the top of the trunk. The leaves are either fan-shaped or feather-shaped, are usually arranged in a spiral at the top of the stem, and have a feature unique among flowering plants: they emerge from the center of the crown like a sword. This sword leaf then expands to reveal a broad, folded surface, which then splits apart into leaflets.

The flowers of the palm are quite inconspicuous, but if you look closely, you will see that they are intricate and varied in their structure. In the past, wind was thought to be responsible for pollination in palms, but we now know that insects such as bees, beetles, weevils, and flies do most of the work.

Key to plate

1: Bacaba
Oenocarpus distichus
Height: 33 feet/10 meters
This tall palm is native to the southern Amazon region. It has long pinnate leaves, meaning they are made up of many leaflets, which are arranged in a single flat plane. The fruits are used to prepare a drink called bacaba wine. Edible oil can also be extracted from its fruit.

2: Coco de mer
Lodoicea maldivica
Height: up to 112 feet/34 meters
Seed
This palm also has some of the longest leaves (up to 33 feet/10 meters). As mentioned above, it also has the largest and heaviest seeds of any plant in the world. These enormous seeds, which usually have 2 lobes, can weigh 40 pounds/18 kilograms and be 12 inches/30 centimeters in diameter.

3: Coconut
Cocos nucifera
Height: up to 98 feet/30 meters
Section through fruit
The fruit of this palm is a fibrous drupe rather than a true nut. A coconut has several layers: the exocarp (or outer husk), the mesocarp (a thick fibrous layer), the endocarp (the hard shell), and the endosperm (the white fleshy part that humans eat). The endosperm is hollow and contains a liquid known as coconut water.

4: Bottle palm
Hyophorbe lagenicaulis
Height: 10–13 feet/3–4 meters
This small palm takes its name from the shape of its trunk. It has a small crown of feather-like leaves, which grow to around 10 feet/3 meters in length. This palm is native to Round Island, Mauritius, where it has recently been rescued from the brink of extinction.

5: Dwarf palmetto
Sabal minor
Height: 3 feet/1 meter
Leaf and fruits
This small fan-leaved species is one of the most cold-tolerant palms. It was used as an important traditional medicine by the Houma people, who dug up the small roots to treat multiple ailments. The juice was rubbed on the eyes to alleviate soreness, while a mixture of the dried roots taken internally corrected high blood pressure and relieved kidney problems. This palm is native to the southern United States.

1

2

3

4

5

The Oil Palm

The oil from the African oil palm tree (*Elaeis guineensis*) is found in cookies, cakes, soaps, lipstick, and many other everyday products throughout the world. Once the oil has been extracted, waste products from the seeds can be used as fertilizer, as fuel for vehicles, and even for road building. Archaeological evidence suggests that our ancestors valued the oil palm too: palm nuts dating back five thousand years have been found on many archaeological digs in western Africa.

In the wild, the oil palm tree grows on the margins of humid forests and along watercourses in drier areas in western and southwestern Africa. Each tree has a single stem, which can grow up to 66 feet/20 meters tall. Leaves are similarly large—often 10–16 feet/3–5 meters long. A young tree may have thirty new leaves each year, an older palm about twenty.

The fruit grows in large bunches, taking five to six months to reach maturity after pollination. The flesh and seed kernel are both rich in oil.

Oil palms have been extensively planted and form an important crop in many parts of Southeast Asia, Africa, and South America. In fact, some plantations in Southeast Asia are so vast they can be seen from space. Managing an industry on this global scale brings challenges

to the local environment, and the areas where the trees grow best include some of the world's most biodiverse and important tropical rain forest. Much rain forest has been cut down to clear the land for palm cultivation, with devastating consequences for local plants and animals, which are being driven to extinction.

But there is a willingness to address this issue. Many of the companies that trade and use the oil palm worldwide have come together in a group called the Roundtable on Sustainable Palm Oil. The group's aim is to ensure that the crop is grown in a sustainable way that does as little damage as possible to tropical rain forest, both now and in the future. There is also increased pressure from consumers on corporations to make products containing sustainable palm oil.

--- *Key to plate* ---

Oil palm
Elaeis guineensis
1: (a) (b) (c) (d) Fruit variously whole and in section
Length: $^3/_4$–2 inches/2–5 centimeters
The fruit is black to orange depending on the stage of ripeness; its flesh consists of 30–60 percent palm oil. The endocarp, or shell, surrounds the seed, or kernel, which contains kernel oil.

2: Male inflorescence (clustered flowers on a stalk)
Length: 14–16 inches/35–40 centimeters

3: Habit (showing the growth and appearance of the plant)
Tree height: up to 66 feet/20 meters
Leaf length: 10–16 feet/3–5 meters

4: Male flower
(a) Flower (b) Cross section through flower
Length: 15–25 millimeters
Each branch of the male inflorescence contains 400 to 1,500 individual flowers.

5: Female inflorescence (clustered flowers on a stalk)
Length: 14–16 inches/35–40 centimeters

Herbaceous Plants

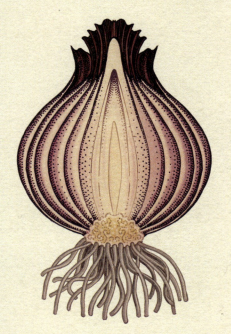

Flower Structure

Flowers are nature's way of showing off. Their dazzling variety of colors, shapes, sizes, and smells is surely one of nature's greatest achievements. The reason plants invest so much flamboyant energy in their flowers lies in their function: it all has to do with reproduction.

Flowers contain male organs, which make pollen, and female organs, which contain egg-bearing ovules. Once fertilized by pollen, the ovules develop into seeds. A new plant then grows from this seed, and the next generation of plants emerges. Some plants have male and female organs on the same flower; others have separate male and female flowers. Plants have evolved a remarkable array of different ways to get the male pollen into the female ovary, and the physical characteristics of a flower tell us how each plant does this.

Plants that use animals for pollination have many ways to lure them in. There are seven main groups of animal pollinators: beetles, flies, bees, butterflies, moths, birds, and bats. Beetles have poor color vision, a good sense of smell, and large bodies. Flowers pollinated by beetles are therefore often plain in color, large enough to support a hefty visitor, and highly scented. Butterflies, on the other hand, have long tongues and good color vision. Flowers pollinated by butterflies are usually brightly colored, with a flat lip to act as a landing platform and a deep tube, which the butterfly reaches into with its long tongue to get nectar. Nectar is a sugary liquid that provides a treat for the pollinator and uses its smell to guide the animal to the right place. The flower's pollen then gets stuck to

the animal and is carried to the next flower, where it fertilizes the female organs.

Other plants, grasses for example, are pollinated by wind. Their flowers do not need color or scent because they don't have to attract animals. Flowers of these plants are usually green, like the rest of the plant, and have small petals, or none. They grow at the top of the plant so that the pollen can blow away freely.

―――――――――――――――― *Key to plate* ――――――――――――――――

1: Creeping buttercup
Ranunculus repens
Height: up to 12 inches/30 centimeters
(a) Cross section through seed.
Each seed contains a small embryo embedded in endosperm. (b) Cross section through flower (c) Stamen—this is the male reproductive part of the flower consisting of a stalk (or filament) that holds the pollen-producing structure (anther) at the top.
The buttercup is a radially symmetrical flower, so it is possible to see many lines of symmetry on the face of the flowers. Buttercups are pollinated by insects.

2: Ryegrass
Lolium perenne
Height: 12–24 inches/
30–60 centimeters
(a) Cross section through flower
(b) Flower clusters on stem
The flowers of this wind-pollinated plant are at the top of the plant, well above the leaves. The stamens, which hold the pollen in the anthers, are long and exposed to the wind.

3. Snapdragon
Antirrhinum majus
Height: up to 12 inches/30 centimeters
(a) Stamen (b) Vertical cross section through ovary (c) Cross section through ovary (d) Cross section through flower showing petal and stamens (e) Vertical cross section through flower
Antirrhinum is a bilaterally symmetrical flower, with a single line of symmetry. It has four different petal shapes: an upper lip, two sides, and a lower lip. This structure creates a tube that the pollinator—a bee—has to force its way inside to reach the nectar. This means that the bee will stand on the flower in a particular position and that pollen placement on the body of the bee will always be in the same area—a very efficient pollination system.

Wild Flowers

Flowering plants that grow without being either planted or altered by human hands are known as wild flowers.

Wild flowers are herbaceous plants. This means that they lack a woody stem that remains above ground all year round. Instead, once they have flowered and shed their seeds, the stem withers and falls over, eventually getting mulched back into the soil. There are three kinds of herbaceous plants: annuals, biennials, and perennials. Annuals live, bloom, and die in the space of a single season. In order to carry on their species to the next generation, they produce large quantities of seeds, which survive in the soil over winter or dry seasons and germinate the following year or when the weather improves. Biennials and herbaceous perennials both leave a living part of themselves below ground, which then grows and flowers in the spring.

The difference between biennials and perennials is length of life. Biennials flower only once, during the plant's second year of life, while perennials go on flowering every year. The part of the plant that remains below ground varies: it can, in some instances, be a bulb (see pages 54–55) or a stem specially thickened to grow below ground (see pages 56–57).

Wild flowers are completely reliant upon nature to disperse their seeds. Annuals disperse and produce seeds only once in their life cycle, so have adapted many methods that maximize their opportunities to do so. Many wild flowers produce vast numbers of seeds to give them the best shot at survival. Many have come up with cunning ways of spreading their seeds. Dandelions, for example, have little feathery parachutes that carry their seeds far away on a breath of wind. Poppy seedcases dry out, then burst, showering seeds as far away from the parent plant as possible.

Key to plate

1: **Black-eyed Susan**
Rudbeckia hirta
Height: 1–3 feet/
30 centimeters–1 meter

2: **Common poppy**
Papaver rhoeas
Height: up to 2 feet/60 centimeters

3: **Germander speedwell**
Veronica chamaedrys
Height: up to 1 foot/30 centimeters

4: **Wild columbine**
Aquilegia canadensis
Height: 2 feet/60 centimeters

5: **Dandelion**
Taraxacum officinale
Height: up to 1 foot/30 centimeters
Fruiting head diameter: 2.5–7.5 centimeters
(a) Flower head (b) Unopened fruiting head (c) Fruiting head (d) Fruiting heads after seed dispersal by wind. One head has four remaining seeds and their "parachutes."
Dandelions look like they have one large yellow flower, but they actually have lots of very small flowers collected into a composite flower head. Each single flower in a head is called a floret.

6: **Common harebell**
Campanula rotundifolia
Height: 4–12 inches/
10–30 centimeters

7: **Japanese anemone**
Anemone hupehensis
Height: 1–3 feet/
30 centimeters–1 meter

8: **Montbretia**
Crocosmia × crocosmiiflora
Height: 1–3 feet/
30 centimeters–1 meter

Cultivated Flowers

People realized a long time ago that plants could be cultivated to help cure illnesses. Medieval doctors believed that plants healed the part of the body they most looked like: black-eyed daisies were thought to be good for disorders of the eye, and broccoli was used to treat diseases of the lungs. Many plants are still cultivated for their medicinal properties (though with a rather greater reliance on scientific evidence!). For example, opium poppies are used to produce two vital painkillers, morphine and codeine. Unfortunately, they are also cultivated to produce heroin, a treacherously addictive drug. This handsome poppy may be the world's most contentious flower.

Other flowers are cultivated for food. The sunflower gives us tasty seeds, which, as well as being eaten whole, can be pressed to release a versatile and flavorsome oil, used in salads, cooking, making margarine, and much more thanks to its high proportion of unsaturated fatty acids. Sunflower oil has other uses, too, including as biofuel (fuel made from plants or other organic matter as opposed to fossil fuels such as crude oil and coal), in soap making, and as a drying oil for paint. The seedcases can also be put to good use after the oil has been extracted, including being mixed with soybean meal to make a protein-rich livestock food. And some Native American peoples, such as the Hidatsa, have long used ground sunflower seeds as an alternative to wheat flour in making bread.

Some flowers are grown for their smell. Roses and lavender were introduced into northern Europe by the Romans. Both are used in the perfume industry—lavender was first cultivated as a scent by the ancient Greeks. Less well known is that the iris is also grown for its scent. To extract an iris's scented oil, its rooting structure, known as a rhizome, needs to be stored for three years. When taken out of storage and squeezed, it exudes a distinctive, butter-colored oil called orris, which smells of violets. Orris also has the unusual property of making other scents smell stronger.

Many plants, of course, are grown simply because they are beautiful. Flowers have been collected from all over the world and cultivated because people enjoy bringing a dash of color or a hint of the exotic into a garden. Hellebores, for example, are native to the Balkans, the Middle East, and China, and have become a favorite with gardeners for their palette of colors and because they flower in both winter and spring.

Key to plate

1: Hellebore
Helleborus sp. hybrid
Height: 1 foot/30 centimeters

2: Common sunflower
Helianthus annuus
Height: up to 10 feet/3 meters
Flower diameter: 4–20 inches/
10–50 centimeters

3: Opium poppy
Papaver somniferum
Height: up to 2 feet/60 centimeters
Seed heads

4: "Old Black Magic" bearded iris
Iris × germanica hybrid
Height: 24–35 inches/
60–90 centimeters

1

2

3

4

Bulbs

If you cut open an onion, you will see many different layers of fleshy material and, right in the middle, a pointed shoot. The outer layer is encased by a thin, paper-like skin. At the base are small, stringy roots. It is a tightly wrapped food parcel, a way of ensuring that the plant survives from one year to the next during periods of drought or cold.

The onion is a bulb. A bulb is an underground shoot surrounded by modified leaves (the layers). It will only grow if it is pointing upward in the ground. When the weather gets bad, the plant effectively goes into a kind of hibernation, or dormancy. The part of the plant sticking up above the ground dies. When the weather warms up or the rains arrive, the shoot grows through the bulb, up through the soil, and out of the earth. The first snowdrops, bluebells, crocuses, and daffodils poking their heads above ground are a familiar sign of spring in temperate regions, and these shoots are soon followed by their abundant flowers.

But even though these plants produce bulbs (and can often survive for years in this form), they still reproduce with seeds. Seeds develop from the fertilized flowers and are dispersed in the usual variety of ways. This is a slow process—it takes up to five years for a mature daffodil plant to develop from a seed because in the first few years, the plant puts most of its energy into growing the bulb.

Plants with fleshy underground parts have been used for food and flavoring for thousands of years. Archaeological evidence indicates that onions, for example, were cultivated in ancient Egypt. Garlic is another bulb that has a long history in food and medicine: 1,500-year-old garlic bulbs were found in the tomb of the Egyptian pharaoh Tutankhamun, and garlic is mentioned in the Bible, the Qur'an, and in many ancient Egyptian, Greek, Indian, and Chinese texts.

Another bulbous plant with a long history in human food is the crocus. In this case, however, it is not the bulb but the pollen-bearing threads called stigmas that are used. These reddish-orange threads are potent and valuable both as a spice for cooking and as a powerful dye for clothes and are more commonly known as saffron. Pound for pound, saffron is the most expensive traded foodstuff in the world. The ancients appreciated its value: the Minoans of Crete grew and traded saffron from around 1550 BCE.

Rather more common, but equally precious in their way, are the humble daffodil and tulip. The tulip has an unwelcome claim to fame. It was the source of the world's first financial crash in Holland in the 1630s. At this time, individual bulbs were traded for the price of four oxen, eight pigs, twelve sheep or a thousand pounds of cheese.

Key to plate

1: **Saffron crocus**
Crocus sativus
Height: 3–7 inches/8–15 centimeters
(a) Vertical cross section through capsule showing developing seeds
(b) Stamen, consisting of filament and anther (c) Stigmas (d) Entire plant

2: **Garlic**
Allium sativum
Height: 12–16 inches/
30–45 centimeters
(a) Stem and bud (b) Flower
(c) Cross section through bulb
(d) Bulb and stem

3: **Tulip**
Tulipa sp.
Height: 6–30 inches/
15–75 centimeters

4: **Red onion**
Allium cepa
Height: 2½–6 feet/
75–180 centimeters
(a) Bulb (b) Vertical cross section through bulb

Belowground Edible Plants

Some plants stay alive during cold and dry seasons by storing starches, proteins, and other nutrients underground in roots, rhizomes, or tubers. Many food crops are provided by these belowground storage organs, including the world's fourth most important food source, the potato, which is a tuber.

Root vegetables include carrots, turnips, rutabagas, parsnips, mangel-wurzel, black salsify, and radishes. Below ground, they grow as a swollen root in a variety of shapes. Leaves grow directly from the aboveground shoulder of this tap root, and there is little or no aboveground stem, only leaves.

By contrast with root vegetables, rhizomes and tubers grow from leafy plants with aboveground stems. Potato plants are leafy, branched green plants with small white flowers. Plants that grow rhizomes and tubers also grow the normal kind of root. Rhizomes often form unusual shapes, such as the knobby underground part of ginger, and are actually roots merged together, usually growing vertically downward in the soil. The word *rhizome* derives from the ancient Greek for "mass of roots."

Tubers include potatoes, sweet potatoes, oca, and yams. A tuber is a short, thick, round stem or root that grows underground, usually as an offshoot from the main stem of the plant. Tubers contain all the necessary parts to produce a new plant. If you leave a potato in a kitchen drawer for too long, for example, it will sprout.

One other belowground food deserves a mention: peanuts. Peanuts are not actually nuts but the seeds of a legume, a plant in the pea family. Peanut flowers grow in clusters on the stems, just above ground. After they are fertilized, a short stalk at the base of the ovary forms, pushing the seed into the soil, where it develops into a mature peanut pod.

Key to plate

1: Potato

Solanum tuberosum

Plant height: up to 3 feet/1 meter

2: Winged yam

Dioscorea alata

Tuber diameter: around 2¹/₂ inches/
6 centimeters

Tuber cut horizontally

Winged yams were domesticated in Southeast Asia and the Pacific but are now eaten in many tropical countries.

3: Beet

Beta vulgaris

Plant height: up to 6¹/₂ feet/2 meters in flower

Root diameter: around 4 inches/
10 centimeters

Root cut horizontally

4: Oca

Oxalis tuberosa

Tuber length: up to 3 inches/
8 centimeters

Tuber

Oca is a crop plant that originated in the Andes, in South America.

5: Radish

Raphanus sativus

Root length: ³/₄ inch–3 feet/
2 centimeters–1 meter

The radish is an edible root vegetable that was domesticated in Europe in pre-Roman times.

6: Carrot

Daucus carota

Root length: 5¹/₂–10 inches/
14–25 centimeters

7: Black salsify

Scorzonera hispanica

Root length: 8 inches–3 feet/
20 centimeters–1 meter

8: Turnip

Brassica rapa

Root diameter: 2–8 inches/
5–20 centimeters

Root

9: Peanut

Arachis hypogaea

Stem height: up to 28 inches/
70 centimeters

Pod length: 1¹/₈–2³/₄ inches/
3–7 centimeters

10: Ginger

Zingiber officinale

Shoot height: up to 4 feet/1.2 meters

The rhizome of ginger comes from Asia.

1

2

8

9

3

6

7

4

5

10

Vines and Creepers

Some herbaceous plants have stems that can barely support their own weight. Instead, they get their structural support from the things around them. These include other plants (usually trees), rocks, and even buildings. The plant drapes itself around and across the supporting structure and climbs toward the sun, spreading its leaves as it goes.

The stems of vines are flexible, allowing for the pulling and twisting needed to grow in any direction dictated by the supporting structure. They have evolved a set of special features to attach themselves to these structures. One is the tendril, a specialized shoot, leaf, or even flower that can search out a likely-looking place to climb and then wrap itself around it. Tendrils often grow like a coiled spring and undergo a 360° clockwise or counterclockwise movement every day. This enables them to reach new supporting structures as the plant grows.

Other vines use adventitious roots, specially adapted roots that grow from the stem and cling to other plants or other surfaces. Many herbaceous vines also have thorns or hooked branches that can grab onto a nearby structure. If herbaceous vines can't find a suitable support structure, they grow horizontally along the ground. These are known as creepers or scramblers.

Key to plate

1: Purple passionflower
Passiflora edulis
Height: 6¹⁄₂ –8 feet/2–2.5 meters
Bud, fruit, leaves, and flower on vine
A fast-growing vine with magnificent purple-and-white flowers up to 4 inches/10 centimeters across, with four yellow anthers containing pollen and an upright sticky yellow stigma. The fruit is similar to a pumpkin or a cucumber. Inside its thick, leathery rind are many seeds embedded in a delicious-tasting, juicy pulp. The pulp consists of the arils, which surround each seed like a sock.

2: Hops
Humulus lupulus
Height: up to 20 feet/6 meters
Fruit on vine
Hops are probably best known for their flowers (sometimes also referred to as seed cones, because of their shape), which are used as the main flavoring ingredient in beer. The earliest evidence of hops used in making beer dates from the ninth century CE.

3: Garden pea
Pisum sativum
Height: 10 feet/3 meters
Pod containing seeds
The pea is one of the most nutritious plants of the legume family. It is cultivated mainly for its edible seeds (the peas), which are rich in protein, vitamins, and minerals. Archaeological evidence found in the Fertile Crescent (the area around modern Israel and Jordan and the Tigris and Euphrates Rivers) indicates that people have been cultivating peas since 8000 BCE. Each pea consists of a seed coat surrounding an embryo with two cotyledons, or embryonic leaves. That's why peas fall into two halves when you open them, just like peanuts. The two halves of a pea or a peanut are the two cotyledons.

4: Pumpkin
Cucurbita pepo
Height: 28 inches/70 centimeters
The pumpkin is one of the oldest domesticated plants. Archaeological sites in northern Mexico have revealed fragments dating to 7000–5500 BCE, and in the southwestern United States to 610 CE. It is an integral part of the squash, beans, and maize diet of many Native American peoples.

5: Sponge gourd
Luffa aegyptiaca
Fruit length: up to 24 inches/61 centimeters long
Fruits, leaf, and tendrils on vine
The sponge gourd is in the cucumber, or Cucurbitaceae, family. The fruit of the sponge gourd is a popular delicacy in China and Vietnam, but in western Europe and the United States, it is best known for a completely different use: scrubbing one's back in the bath. The luffa (or loofah) fruit is very fibrous when ripe. Remove the flesh, and you have an excellent scrubbing sponge.

6: Dodder laurel
Cassytha ciliolata
Vine length: can form dense mats of stems up to 16 feet/5 meters tall
(a) Vine and fruits (b) Vertical cross section through fruit
This is a parasitic vine (see pages 86–87). This means that it not only uses another plant for support, but it also exploits it as a source of nutrition. Dodder laurel produces small, red, fleshy fruits that are eaten by birds and sometimes humans.

1

2

3

4

5

6a

6b

Environment: Alpine Plants

Alpine plants don't just grow in the Alps. They can survive anywhere in the world with the right conditions. These include very low temperatures, often below 32°F/0°C for months at a time; dryness; high levels of ultraviolet radiation; and a very short growing season (often less than three months of the year). These conditions present alpine plants with three big challenges to their survival.

First, in the highest areas where plants grow, there is usually very little soil, and what there is can be loose and rocky. Plants need a way to anchor themselves in this environment. Some plants, such as creeping avens, form long runners that grow over the top of stony soil and tie down loose soil, or scree. Others, such as purple saxifrage, form dense cushions of growth in the cracks of rocks; the cushions protect the plant's roots and insulate it against the cold.

The second challenge is the harsh climate, in particular the frequent alternation of freeze and thaw. This is a challenge for young plants and demands special germination strategies. One of these is the process known as vivipary: seeds germinate while still attached to the mother plant, allowing each generation to protect the next until it reaches maturity. This produces a tufty appearance, common in alpine grasses such as *Poa alpina*. Another way plants protect themselves from the cold is to have part of their structure permanently underground, with an aboveground part that shows only when the weather is suitable. Common moonwort, an alpine fern, is an example of this adaptation.

The third challenge for these plants is that the growing season is short and pollinators are rare. Adaptations include early flowering, large flowers, and self-pollination. The alpine snowbell, for example, is among the first species to emerge after winter, so it makes use of the earliest pollinators without competition. The stemless gentian, by contrast, puts its energies into producing a large flower. This makes it attractive to bumblebees (which are well adapted to cold places because of their size). Other alpine plants self-pollinate. The long-flowered primrose, for example, is sometimes pollinated by hawkmoths, but can also pollinate itself in their absence.

Key to plate

1: **Alpine meadow grass**
Poa alpina
Height: 6 inches/15 centimeters

2: **Creeping avens**
Geum reptans
Height: 4 inches/10 centimeters

3: **Alpine snowbell**
Soldanella alpina
Height: 4 inches/10 centimeters

4: **Long-flowered primrose**
Primula halleri
Height: 8 inches/20 centimeters

5: **Common moonwort**
Botrychium lunaria
Height: 4 inches/10 centimeters

6: **Purple saxifrage**
Saxifraga oppositifolia
Height: 1 1/2 inches/4 centimeters

7: **Stemless gentian**
Gentiana acaulis
Height: 4 inches/10 centimeters

Gallery 5

Grasses, Cattails, Sedges, and Rushes

Grasses
Crops
Cattails, Sedges, and Rushes

Grasses

The grass family (Poaceae) contains more than ten thousand species, including some of the most important plants for humans. Three grasses—maize, wheat, and rice (see pages 66–67)—account for more than 50 percent of the world's food. Grasses grow almost everywhere, from the tropics to the cold polar regions. There are, for example, only two species of flowering plants in the Antarctic and one of them is a grass (*Deschampsia antarctica*). It is estimated that more than 25 percent of the world's surface is covered with grass—a remarkable fact considering that grasses are one of the most recent groups of plants to evolve. The first evidence of grass in the fossil record appears around 60 million years ago, about the same time as the first appearance of many hoofed mammals, including horses.

Grasses are mostly herbaceous and have long, narrow leaves and hollow, jointed stems. They can grow very tall, like bamboos, or almost flat to the ground. Many grasses spread by growing horizontal underground stems called rhizomes. The aboveground stems are called stolons. New grass shoots can emerge from either stolons or rhizomes. Unlike many plants, the growing point is not at the tip of the grass but near its base or even below ground. This means that grasses are able to withstand grazing, burning, and heavy pounding in public parks and on sports fields without damage to the growing point. Many grasses can survive drought because their extensive root systems store large amounts of food.

Key to plate

1: **Taiwanese giant bamboo**
Dendrocalamus latiflorus
(a) Flowers (b) Leaves (c) Stem
Height: 46–82 feet/14–25 meters
This giant species of bamboo grows throughout China and eastern Asia. It is found in dense clumps in tropical and subtropical environments. Its light, hollow stems are useful for all sorts of things including timber for building, water pipes, furniture, and even musical instruments. One giant panda can eat between 25–85 pounds/11–39 kilograms of bamboo shoots every day.

2: **Pink muhly grass**
Muhlenbergia capillaris
Height and spread: 24–35 inches/60–90 centimeters
Flowers on stems
Often known as pink hair grass, this plant grows across the United States from Massachusetts to Florida and Texas, and all across the prairies.

3: **Blue grama**
Bouteloua gracilis
Height: 6–20 inches/15–50 centimeters
Flowers on stem
This grass is sometimes called

mosquito grass, from its distinctive arrangement of seed spikes. These hang down from one side of the flowering stem and look like mosquito larvae. It grows in the plains and open rocky woodlands of the western United States.

4: **Purple moor grass**
Molinia caerulea
Height: 1–3 feet/30 centimeters–1 meter
Stem diameter: 2–3 millimeters
Cross section through stem

5: **Red fescue**
Festuca rubra
Height: $^3/_4$–8 inches/2–20 centimeters
(a) Junction between a leaf blade (above) and leaf sheath surrounding the stem (below) (b) Stem
This grass is found in lawns, parks, and sports fields throughout the Western Hemisphere. It spreads by long, horizontal underground shoots called rhizomes. Some of these have been estimated to be up to 820 feet/250 meters long and more than four hundred years old.

6: **Bermuda grass**
Cynodon dactylon
Height: up to 10 inches/25 centimeters
Seeds at the top of a stem
Not all grasses are beneficial. This one is listed as one of the most damaging weeds to agriculture and the environment in the world. Originally from Africa, it grows very fast and can rapidly take over new areas with dense mats of growth that can stifle everything else.

7: **Sugarcane**
Saccharum officinarum
Height: 10–20 feet/3–6 meters
(a) Stem (b) Flowers
Sugarcane probably originated in New Guinea. Christopher Columbus introduced it into the Americas from Europe on his second expedition (1493–1496). Sugarcane provides around 70 percent of the world's sugar and is grown mainly in tropical but also in some subtropical areas. India and Brazil produce about half the world's cane sugar.

1a   *1b*   2   *7b*

3   4   *7a*

5b   6

5a   *1c*

Crops

More than half the world's food comes from the seeds of just three crops: the edible cereal grains corn, wheat, and rice. All are members of the grass family. Corn, or maize (*Zea mays*), is Earth's most produced crop by volume at over a billion tons per year. It is a staple human food and is used as biofuel and to feed farm animals. All this derived from a single domestication event in the Tehuacán Valley in Mexico about nine thousand years ago. This early crop was a small, scrubby plant, a subspecies known as *Zea mays* ssp. *parviglumis*. Cultivation spread through Central and South America. The Aztecs prized corn so highly that it had its own god, Centeotl. Between one thousand and five hundred years ago, it became established in what is now the southeastern United States. Explorers brought it to Europe beginning in the late fifteenth century.

The wheat we know today was first cultivated around ten thousand years ago in the eastern Mediterranean. The evolution of modern wheat was part luck, part design. The first wheats grown for food were einkorn (*Triticum monococcum*) and emmer wheat (*Triticum dicoccon*). Emmer wheat is a naturally occurring combination, or hybridization, of two species of grass. When emmer hybridized further with goat grass (*Aegilops tauschii*), farmers had a high-yield, high-protein variety—modern bread wheat (*Triticum aestivum*).

Asian rice (*Oryza sativa*) probably originated in Southeast Asia. Its wild ancestor, *Oryza rufipogon,* still grows there today. Records of domesticated rice in southern China have been found dating back to around 6000 BCE. Other members of the grass family that give us grains include barley, millet, and oats.

6   7   8

Key to plate

1: Teosinte
Zea mays ssp. *parviglumis*
Height: 20–36 inches/
50 centimeters–1 meter
This is thought to be the wild crop
relative of *Zea mays*. It has no cob.

2: Corn
Zea mays
Height: 10–40 feet/3–12 meters
The tall stem of *Zea mays* carries
both male and female reproductive
parts. The male part is at the top
of the plant in the form of hair-like
tassels, the female about halfway
down, surrounded by several layers of
leaves, commonly called husks. Once
fertilized, this female part develops
into the familiar cob, which we eat.
It contains about six hundred fruits,
or kernels.

3: Goat grass
Aegilops tauschii
Height: 1 foot/30 centimeters
The flowers of this grass are small and
hidden inside green modified leaves

called lemma and palea. Every lemma
has a bristle on its end called an awn,
which attaches itself to passing animals
so the grain can spread.

4: Emmer wheat
Triticum dicoccon
Height: up to 5 feet/1.5 meters
The name *dicoccon* refers to the
fact that this species produces two
grains inside every spikelet, or unit of
flowering structure. An ear of wheat is
made up of spikelets packed together
with modified leaves to protect the
developing grains.

5: Bread wheat
Triticum aestivum
Height: 26–36 inches/
65 centimeters–1 meter
Bread wheat produces two to four
grains in every spikelet, so it has better
productivity than emmer wheat. Some
varieties have awns (bristles) and some
do not.

6: Rice
Oryza sativa
Height: up to 16 feet/5 meters
Rice produces grains, the central part
of which (the endocarp), provide a
staple food for millions of people.
It grows with its roots in deep water.

7: Oats
Avena sativa
Height: 16 inches–6 feet/
40 centimeters–1.8 meters
This member of the grass family
produces hanging clusters of flowering
structures surrounded by modified
leaves called glumes. The structures are
easier to see than in other members
of the grass family because the
spikelets are larger, at around
1 inch/2.5 centimeters long.

8: Pearl millet
Pennisetum glaucum
Height: 5–10 feet/1.5–3 meters
This crop is particularly popular
in drought-affected areas of India
and Africa.

Cattails, Sedges, and Rushes

In ponds and wetlands all over the world, cattails, sedges, and rushes grow along the edge of the water. These tall plants look a bit like grasses, but they are not grasses and are actually not related to one another.

Cattails belong to the Typhaceae family. They have a distinctive sausage-shaped structure toward the top of the growing stem, which is composed of hundreds of tiny flowers packed tightly together. Above it, on a spike, is the male part of the plant, containing the pollen. When the tiny seeds are mature, the sausage-shaped structure begins to fray open, and the seeds, attached to silky threads, are dispersed by the wind.

Sedges belong to the Cyperaceae family. While grasses have long, cylindrical, hollow stems (see pages 64–65), sedges have triangular stems, which are filled with a sticky substance called pith. Humans have used sedges for thousands of years for food, fuel, and paper making. Several species of Cyperaceae produce edible tubers, including the delicately flavored Chinese water chestnut. The most well known member of the sedge family is probably papyrus, which the ancient Egyptians made into paper, as well as a firm, flexible outer skin for boats.

Rushes belong to the Juncaceae family. They have distinctive flowers, scale-like in appearance, made up of three petals and three sepals (leaf-like structures that protect the flower bud) arranged alternately in a symmetrical ring. It is one of very few flowers in nature that is brown. Rushes have long, hairless cylindrical stem-like leaves and a round hollow stem.

Key to plate

1: **Cattail**
Typha latifolia
Height: up to 8 feet/2.5 meters
(a) Flower head (b) Cut-away stem
Cattails have been used in some parts of the world to decontaminate waterways because they can absorb pollutants without dying.

2: **Papyrus**
Cyperus papyrus
Height: up to 16 feet/5 meters
(a) Leaves and flowers
(b) Cut-away stem
This fast-growing sedge is native to Africa but is cultivated widely. Papyrus,

a paper-like material made from the pith in the stem of the plant, was first manufactured in Egypt as far back as the fourth millennium BCE. To make papyrus, the outer part of the stem is removed and the pith inside is cut into strips. The strips are lined up side by side on a hard surface, then a second layer of strips is placed over them at right angles. These two layers are then hammered into a single sheet, which is dried, flattened with heavy stones, and polished.

3: **Heath rush**
Juncus squarrosus
Height: up to 20 inches/
50 centimeters
(a) Stigma branches (top),
style (middle stem-like section),
and ovary (bottom)
(b) Flower (c) Stem and flowers
This rush grows in wet, peaty heathlands and moorland.

Orchids and Bromeliads

Orchids
The Christmas Star Orchid
Bromeliads

Orchids

Orchids provide some striking statistics. There are around 28,000 species, making Orchidaceae the largest family of herbaceous flowering plants in the world. Typically, each species is highly localized and adapted very precisely to its particular circumstances. Orchids grow around the world and in a variety of habitats, from the dark floor of the rain forest to the tall tops of tropical trees.

Over half of orchids are epiphytes. These are commonly known as air plants because they get their support from another plant and grow high up in its branches with their roots sticking into the air. The roots absorb the necessary water and nutrients from mist, moisture, dust, and debris that swirl around and collect on them in the treetops. Ground-dwelling orchids can often adapt to unappealing environments like boggy marshlands.

Orchids are the actors of the plant world, and the weird and varied shapes of the flowers reflect many highly specialized pollination systems. Many mimic the insects that pollinate them, and these adaptations are deliberate ploys to attract a pollinator. The insect is lured with what looks like the promise of an encounter with an insect of the opposite sex. The bee orchid (*Ophrys apifera*) is an example of this. Some, such as *Catasetum fimbriatum,* have mechanisms for shooting pollen at their pollinator!

Orchids' shapes, colors, and scents have made them prize exhibits in greenhouses and as houseplants for centuries. In the 1800s, plant hunters drove many of the rarest species close to extinction. Most plants are now cultivated from seed. However, wild orchids are still endangered because of the small numbers of individual plants in each species.

Key to plate

1: Lady Ackland's Cattleya
Cattleya aclandiae
Height: 8–10 inches/20–25 centimeters
Flower
This species is native to Bahia, in Brazil. Its sweet smell attracts large bees that expect to find nectar, even though none is present.

2: Fringed catasetums
Catasetum fimbriatum
Height: 24–30 inches/
61–76 centimeters
Flowers on stem
This orchid's flower has two small hairs close to its lip. When a bee knocks into them, it triggers a forceful release of pollen.

3: Vanilla
Vanilla pompona
Height: up to 51 feet/15.5 meters
Flowers, buds, and leaf
Humans actually eat some orchids. The vanilla pod comes from the vanilla bean, which is the cured unripe fruit

of this orchid. Up to 75 percent of the world's vanilla comes from *Vanilia planifolia*, native to Mexico and grown in Madagascar, the Comoros, and Réunion.

4: Umbrella orchid
Trichosalpinx rotundata
Height: 2–3 inches/5–8 centimeters
Leaf and flowers
The tiny flowers of this Central American orchid are produced on the underside of the round leaf, which, like a miniature umbrella, protects the flies that pollinate it from the frequent rains.

5: Bee orchid
Ophrys apifera
Height: 10–15 inches/
25–38 centimeters
Flowers on stem
Ophrys apifera has furry brown-and-yellow stripes, like a female bee. When a hapless male bee tries to mate with the flower, he gets covered in pollen.

6: Rothschild's slipper orchid
Paphiopedilum rothschildianum
Height: 3–5 feet/1–1.5 meters in flower
This species grows only on the lower slopes of Mount Kinabalu, in Borneo.

7: Vampire orchid
Dracula vampira
Height: 8–12 inches/20–30 centimeters
Flower
This dramatic-looking native of Ecuador is pollinated by small mushroom-eating gnats. It produces a fragrance that mimics the smell of a mushroom, deceiving the gnats as they wander around the flower looking for food.

8: **Masdevallia stumpflei**
Height: 8–14 inches/20–35 centimeters
in flower
Flower
This species, thought to be native to Peru, was only discovered in 1979, growing in a greenhouse in Germany. It has never been found in the wild.

The Christmas Star Orchid

This beautiful white orchid comes from Madagascar. It grows up to 3 feet/1 meter high and is epiphytic, growing off tree trunks. It has long, narrow leathery leaves and large white flowers. It holds its nectar in a nectar spur, a long, elongated hollow tube (up to 1 foot/30 centimeters long) extending behind the flower.

This is an enigmatic beauty with a fascinating past. It was discovered in Madagascar by a French explorer who brought it back to the Jardin des Plantes, in Paris, in 1802. Later, some flowers were sent to the English Royal Botanic Gardens at Kew. Kew's director, Joseph Hooker, displayed some of his new acquisitions proudly in his splendid greenhouse and, in 1862, sent a few to his friend the naturalist Charles Darwin, most famous today for his theory of evolution. Darwin was intrigued: "I have just received such a Box full with the astounding *Angraecum sesquipedale* with a nectary a foot long. Good Heavens what insect can suck it?" he wrote to Hooker. There must, thought Darwin, be an as yet unknown species of insect with a proboscis, or tongue, almost a foot long, able to access the flower's nectar. Not for the first time, people thought Darwin was, to put it politely, being a little fanciful. But in 1903, more than four decades later, he was proved right. A new species of hawkmoth was discovered that has a proboscis long enough to reach into the nectar spur of the Christmas star orchid. Eventually, after patient observation, it was observed in the wild doing exactly that.

--- *Key to plate* ---

1: **The Christmas star orchid**
Angraecum sesquipedale
Height: up to 3 feet/1 meter
Nectar spur: up to 1 foot/
30 centimeters long

2: Xanthopan morganii **ssp.**
praedicta
This is the Christmas star orchid's
exceptionally long-tongued pollinator.

Bromeliads

Plants from the Bromeliaceae, or bromeliad, family are found almost exclusively in North and South America. Only one species of bromeliad, *Pitcairnia feliciana,* is known to grow wild outside of America. It lives in western Africa. Nearly three thousand different species exist in almost every environment in the Americas, from rain forests to dry zones in the tropics, and from mountainside cloud forests to arid deserts. Remarkably, it is believed that all bromeliads evolved around the same time, between 60 and 30 million years ago.

Bromeliads grow as a rosette of leaves, usually without a stem, a unique and striking feature. In some species, known as tank bromeliads, these stiff overlapping leaves are capable of holding rainwater in their center, giving the plant a source of moisture in the dry season. This creates a damp, well-protected ecosystem for tree frogs, snails, flatworms, tiny crabs, salamanders, algae, and insect larvae.

The leaves of bromeliads tend to be patterned — striped, spotted, or banded — in a variety of rich colors, including white, cream, yellow, purple, red, silver, maroon, and black. As well as showy leaves, bromeliads also have very pretty and brightly colored flowers, which usually grow on spikes. Some of these spikes stick up straight out of the leaf rosette, up to 33 feet/10 meters high. Others are droopy, hanging down lower than the plant itself. Over half of bromeliads grow as epiphytes, anchoring themselves to other plants, often on the branches of trees. Hundreds of individual bromeliad plants have been seen growing on a single branch of a tropical tree; branches sometimes break under the weight. Other species of bromeliad grow on the ground, with their roots in the soil. Others are saxicolous, meaning that they grow on rocks.

Bromeliads were well known to the Inca, Aztec, and Maya peoples, who used them for food, fiber, and ceremonies. They appeared in Europe when Christopher Columbus unloaded a particularly tasty variety — the pineapple — on his return from his 1496 voyage.

Key to plate

1: **Red pineapple**
Ananas bracteatus
Plant height: 4 feet/1.2 meters
Fruit

2: **Common pineapple**
Ananas comosus
Plant height: 3–6 ¹/₂ feet/1–2 meters
Fruit
The pineapple is the only member

of the Bromeliaceae family that is still economically important. A pineapple is not a simple fruit but consists of many fruits in one large, fleshy structure. In tropical America, where pineapples are native, tapirs feed on wild pineapples and help disperse their seeds. Cultivated pineapples are bred to be seedless.

3: **Puya berteroniana**
Height: 10 feet/3 meters
Flowers

4: **King of the bromeliads**
Vriesea hieroglyphica
Height: 2 feet/60 centimeters
Leaf length: up to 3 feet/1 meter

Adapting to Environments

Succulents and Cacti

The term succulents refers to plants that have a set of features that allow them to live in some of the driest environments on Earth. These features include specialized plant tissues, which absorb and hold moisture so that photosynthesis (which requires water) can still occur even during droughts. Succulents also tend to have tough coverings on the stem to support the weight of the stored water. The leaves are thick and leathery to the touch, with a waxlike whitish covering that helps to reduce water loss from evaporation and damage to leaves from fierce sun. Some succulents have long white hairs to protect them from the sunlight and, just as important, from subzero desert nights.

During a drought, succulents are sometimes the only green things that grow. Naturally, this makes them tempting to hungry herbivores. They have evolved several defensive adaptions. Some succulents have a bitter taste, while others have sharp, prickly spines. Perhaps the most extraordinary method of defense is camouflage. Stone plants, for instance, look like pebbles—until they burst into flower, producing a showy bloom like a big daisy.

Cacti have many of the adaptations listed above but instead of leaves, they have sharp spines, which are in fact a highly modified form of a leaf. This means that in cacti, all the photosynthesis is carried out in the stem. As well as being a highly effective defense against herbivores, the spines also break up the air flow around the plant, reducing water loss from evaporation.

Key to plate

1: Zebra cactus
Haworthias attenuata
Height: up to 20 inches/
50 centimeters
These small cacti, which are native to southern Africa, have distinctive triangular leaves and a white pattern resembling zebra stripes.

2: Ball cacti
Parodia magnifica
Height: 2³/₄–6 inches/7–15 centimeters
Ball cacti usually grow in clumps with all the plants facing in the same direction, hence their nickname "compass cacti."

3: Jelly bean plant
Sedum pachyphyllum
Height: up to 10 inches/25 centimeters
Leaves on stem
The leaves of this plant, which is native to Mexico, look like jelly beans but are not edible. The round shape of the leaves (like string-of-pearls, number 4) helps reduce the amount of sunlight absorbed by the leaf.

4: String-of-pearls
Senecio rowleyanus
Length of trailing stems: up to 35 inches/90 centimeters
Leaves on vine
This succulent is a member of the daisy family (Asteraceae) that grows in the desert of South Africa. Each "pearl" is a leaf.

5: Prickly pear
Opuntia engelmannii
Height: 10 feet/3 meters
Prickly pears produce delicious, sweet fruit. The large, flat pads are the plant stems, and the sharp spines are modified leaves. Prickly pears are the most wide-ranging cacti and occur throughout South America and as far north as Canada.

6: African milk tree
Euphorbia trigona
Height: up to 9 feet/2.7 meters
Euphorbias and cacti look very similar but are not related. This plant is a euphorbia from Central Africa. It has a dark green upright stem shaped into a series of ridges. Thorns approximately

5 millimeters long grow in pairs on two of the ridges, and small drop-shaped leaves grow between the two thorns.

7: Crow's claw cactus
Ferocactus latispinus
Height: up to 1 foot/30 centimeters
This species of barrel cactus is native to Mexico and has spines up to 2 inches/5 centimeters long.

8: Stone plant
Lithops hookeri
Height: up to 2 inches/5 centimeters
Stone plants grow partially buried in the ground; they are native to Namibia and South Africa.

9: *Echeveria laui*
Height: up to 6 inches/15 centimeters
(a) Sprouting leaf (b) Entire plant
The bluish color of this plant's leaves is due to pigments that help the plant control the sunlight absorbed for photosynthesis. The plant is covered in a layer of powdery wax that protects the succulent tissue beneath. It is native to Mexico.

1

2

3

4

5

6

7

8

9a

9b

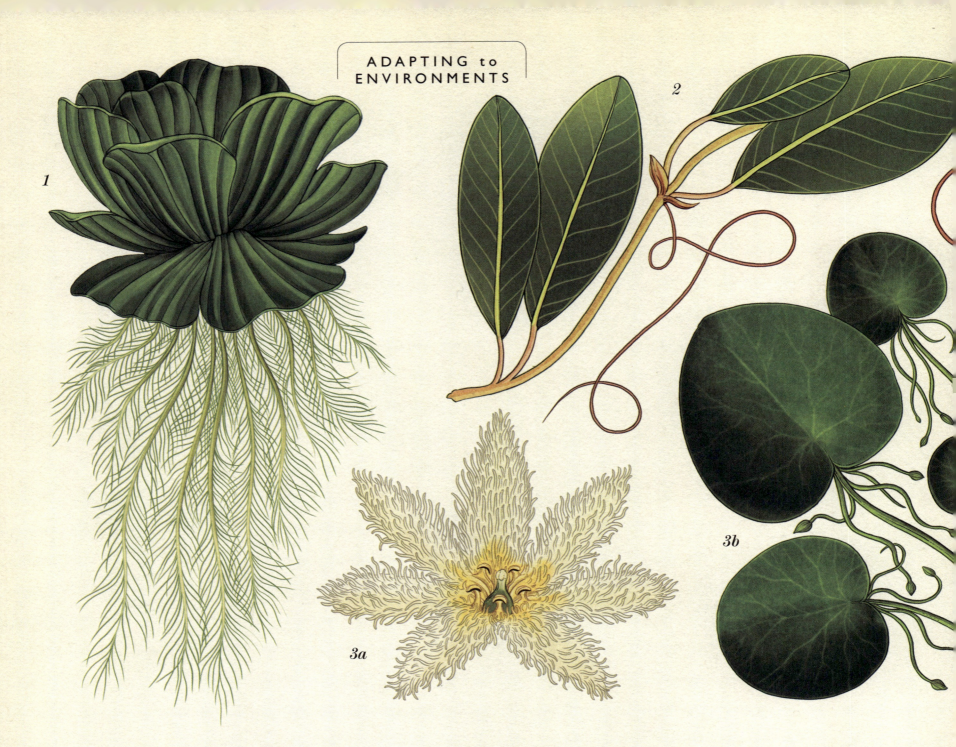

Aquatic Plants

Aquatic plants grow in water or in soil that is permanently wet. They include many plants seen in previous galleries: algae, mosses, liverworts, hornworts, club mosses, horsetails, and many ferns, all of which reproduce without flowers; as well as cattails, sedges, and rushes, which have their roots in water and do reproduce with flowers. But there is another group of flowering aquatic plants with a very unusual ability: they grow entirely underwater, or partially below the water with just the leaves and flowers on the surface.

Water is denser than air, so these aquatic plants get more support from their environment than land plants do. Their tissue is less firm than that of land plants, and they have flexible stems that can move with the water. They also have air-filled cavities to give buoyancy and leaves with little or none of the waxy covering other plants use to minimize water loss through evaporation. Permanently submerged leaves tend to be long, thin, and divided many times, which offers less resistance to water currents and presents more surface area for absorbing carbon dioxide. Leaves that float tend to be round and smooth, also offering less resistance to water currents, and they also tend to have long stalks that move up and down if the water level changes. Specialized air pockets called lacunae give added buoyancy.

Flowers can be produced underwater or on or above the surface Above-surface flowers tend to be pollinated by wind or insects. Those below the surface disperse their pollen by water. This is not reliable, since pollen can be swept away, so most aquatic plants

reproduce asexually as well, by growing rhizomes in the soil beneath the water that then send up new shoots a little way from the parent plant. Eventually these detach and a new plant is created, genetically identical to its parent.

<hr />

Key to plate

1: Water lettuce
Pistia stratiotes
Height: 6 inches/15 centimeters
Water lettuce grows in subtropical fresh waterways. Its free-floating roots are well adapted to absorbing nutrients from flowing water.

2: Paddle weed
Halophila ovalis
Leaf length: up to 1 inch/
2.5 centimeters
Leaves and stem
This saltwater sea grass lives in mud flats and sandbanks around reefs, estuaries, and deltas. Its meadow-like growth provides an ideal grazing ground for the marine mammal the dugong, giving the plant its other name, dugong grass.

3: Water snowflake
Nymphoides indica
Leaf diameter: 2 inches/5 centimeters
(a) Flower (b) Leaves
These five-lobed flowers grow above the water. Their name comes from the delicate hair-like growths on the petals. *Nymphoides* are also known as floating heart plants.

4: Common eelgrass
Zostera marina
Leaf length: usually 8–20 inches/
20–50 centimeters but sometimes up to 6¹/₂ feet/2 meters
A sea grass, also known as sea wrack. It can live in cool waters near ocean coasts and has become the most widespread marine flowering plant in the Northern Hemisphere, growing

along the coasts of Europe, North America, and the Arctic. It is the only sea grass found in Iceland.

5: American featherfoil
Hottonia inflata
Height: 1–2 feet/30–60 centimeters
This freshwater aquatic plant, native to the eastern United States, grows in swamps and ditches as well as in ponds that have been excavated and dammed by beavers. It has a basal root, which burrows into the mud below the water, and feathery roots, which float free in the water.

The Amazon Water Lily

The Amazon water lily, *Victoria amazonica,* is a giant waterborne plant, with leaves that grow to 8 feet/2.5 meters wide. It fascinated and intrigued the first Europeans who saw it, including Robert Schomburgk, who found what he described as this "vegetable wonder" in South America in 1837. Schomburgk was determined to bring a specimen back to show the Royal Geographical Society in London, but the leaf was bigger than his canoe. Undaunted, he packed a bud and a small piece of leaf into a barrel full of salt water and set off back down the river to get his finds onto the ship bound for England. It was Schomburgk's idea to name the discovery after the then princess Victoria, who had become queen by the time he returned home.

England's climate is, of course, very different from South America's. Botanists and gardeners there tried to get water lily seeds to germinate and grow, but couldn't. Two rivals in particular went head to head: Joseph Paxton, head gardener to the duke of Devonshire, and William Hooker, director of the Royal Botanic Gardens at Kew. Hooker was the first to grow plants from seed, but Paxton realized that he needed to create an environment similar to the Amazonian jungle to get them to flower, which he was able to do in a specially built greenhouse and won the race. "My Lord Duke, Victoria has Shewn Flower!" he wrote in triumph to his employer in 1846. "No account can give a fair idea of the grandeur of its appearance." Paxton went on to become a leading architect of greenhouses. He was fascinated by the Amazon water lily's network of ribs that supports its leaves, and he copied it in iron and glass, most notably in the Crystal Palace, built for London's Great Exhibition of 1851.

The leaves of the Amazon water lily first appear as spiny heads poking up through the water but expand rapidly across the water's surface, growing at a rate of up to 20 inches/50 centimeters a day. On the red underside of the leaves, the ribs are covered in many sharp spines—a defense mechanism against fish and Amazonian manatees. Air trapped in the spaces between the ribs enables the leaves to float. The plant's enormous white flowers have a scent like pineapple. They open in the evening, giving off heat, which attracts pollinating beetles. They then turn a pale pink and close for the night.

Key to plate

1: **Amazon water lily**
Victoria amazonica
Leaf diameter: up to 8 feet/2.5 meters
Leaf

The leaves of the Amazon water lily are so buoyant that they can easily support the weight of a child—something Paxton proved

by getting his daughter to lie down on a tin tray on a leaf.

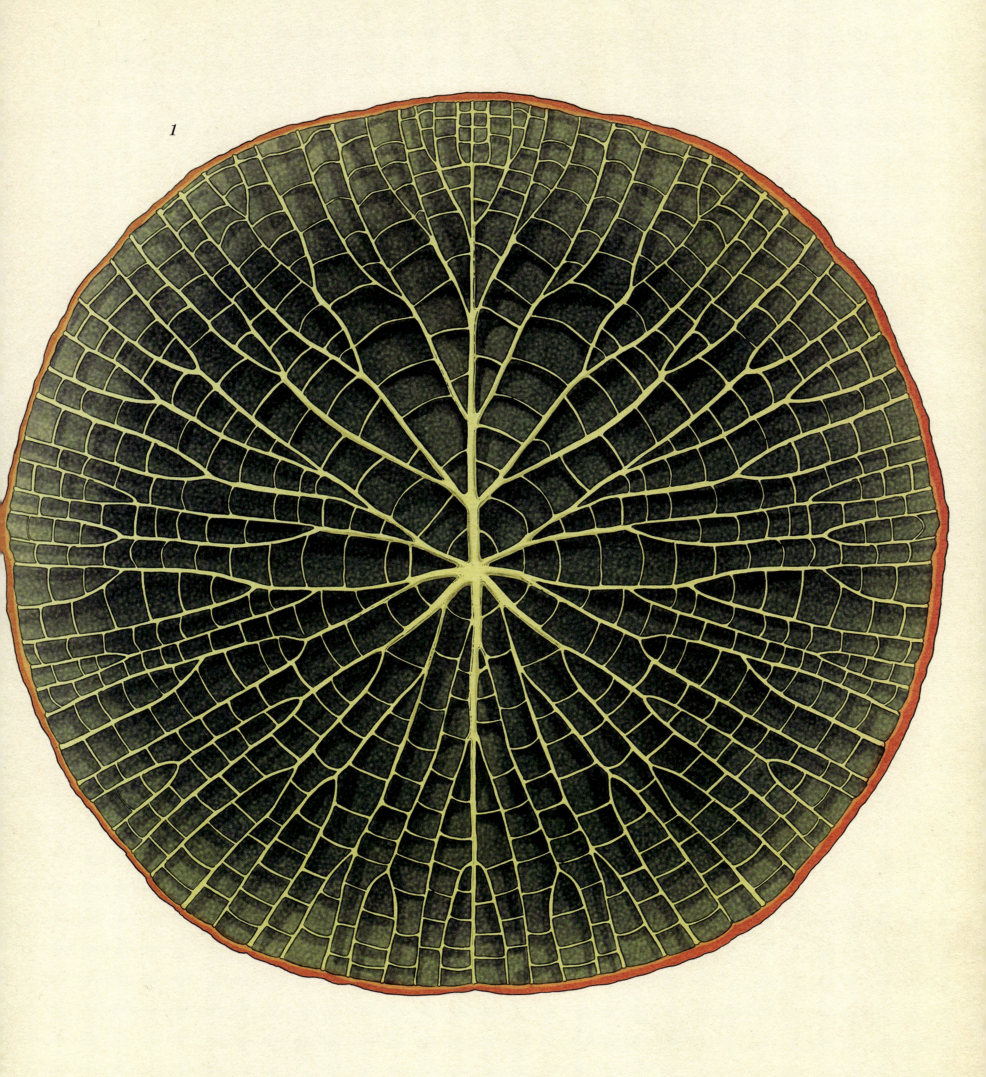

1

Parasitic Plants

All plants need food, water, and nutrients. Most get their own from sun, rain, and soil. Some, however, use other plants to meet their needs. These are called parasitic plants. Some become entirely reliant upon another plant. In other cases, the parasitic plant relies on another plant for some things but continues to make its own food as well.

A parasitic plant taps the resources of its host via a modified root called a haustorium. The haustorium produces a special glue to fix itself to the root or shoot of the host plant. It then penetrates the wall of the host plant and links up with the host plant's vascular system. Once in place, the haustorium acts as a pipeline, taking water and nutrients directly from the host into the parasite plant.

The process of attachment to a host plant starts when a parasitic plant's seed germinates. Parasitic plants usually produce many small seeds. These are dispersed into the soil or directly onto the host stem, usually via bird droppings. When a seed picks up a chemical signal, which tells them they have landed near a suitable host, the seed begins to germinate and the haustorium starts to grow as a root. Once the haustorium is connected, the host plant provides the vital ingredients for growth and the mature parasite plant develops, often with leaves and flowers.

Some parasitic plants have an extremely unusual feature—they're not green. This is because their host does their photosynthesizing for them, so they lose their chlorophyll, the green pigment necessary for photosynthesis.

Key to plate

1: **Stinking corpse flower**
Rafflesia arnoldii
Diameter: up to 3 feet/1 meter
Flower
This flower has two claims to fame. The first is that it produces the largest individual flower on Earth. The other is that it stinks, emitting a smell that is similar to rotting flesh. This plant is often found growing on the bark of trees and vines in the grape family (Vitaceae) in the rain forests of Borneo and Sumatra. The plant is mostly hidden within the host plant until the flower breaks through its bark.

2: **Mistletoe**
Viscum album
Height: up to 3 feet/1 meter
Leaves and stems with fruit
As well as being a Christmas favorite, mistletoe is an example of a parasitic plant that grows mostly on the surface of the host plant. Mistletoe is

found growing on trees and shrubs in wooded habitats from the tropics to temperate regions. It depends on its host for water and mineral nutrients but photosynthesizes to create its own carbohydrates, so keeps its green stems and leaves. Mistletoe can sometimes become so abundant that it causes a serious problem for their host.

3: **Asiatic witchweed**
Striga asiatica
Height: 6–16 inches/
15–30 centimeters
Flowers, leaves, and stems
This parasitic weed has wreaked havoc in agricultural fields in many parts of the semiarid regions of Africa, India, and the United States. It threatens important crop species, including corn, rice, and sugarcane (see pages 64–67). It drops its seeds into the soil, where they react to a chemical signal from the host plant by ceveloping the haustorium to tap into its water

and nutrients. When the seedlings emerge from below ground, they produce leaves and flowers, so the parasite appears to be growing happily alongside the host. In fact, below ground, it is sucking away its vital nutrients.

4: **European dodder**
Cuscuta europaea
Flower head diameter: 6 millimeters
Stem, flowers, and buds
European dodder causes significant damage to crops. It is a parasitic vine found throughout the Northern Hemisphere, and it is a serious weed. Its stems twine around the shoots and leaves of host plants, choking them. Because it relies on its host for photosynthesis, it has tiny leaves and almost no chlorophyll, so the stems are not green but a vivid orange.

Carnivorous Plants

These fascinating plants catch and eat live prey—mostly insects, though some also feed on spiders, small crabs, mites, and small single-cell organisms called protozoans. Their taste for flesh comes from their need for nitrogen. All plants need nitrogen to make chlorophyll (the green pigment used in photosynthesis) and proteins. Carnivorous plants tend to grow in boggy or other acidic environments with little nitrogen, so they need to get it from a different source. They produce special chemicals that digest and then release the nitrogen from a victim. But they have to catch their prey first. Carnivorous plants have two main ways of doing this: passive and active traps.

Passive traps don't involve any active movement by the plant. The prey is lured by the sweet smell of nectar. It then finds itself trapped. There are several different ways a plant does this. One is by sticking the visitor's feet and body to the leaf with a kind of glue produced by hairs on the leaf's surface. Once stuck, the prey is then digested by chemicals secreted by other hairs on the leaf. Another way is to tip the prey into a pitfall trap. These plants grow modified leaves that look like small cauldrons and are filled with digestive chemicals. The sloping upper part is waxy: the victim slips, loses its footing, and in it goes. Downward-pointing hairs or slippery scales then keep it from getting out again.

Active traps involve movement. There are two main types of active trap. The first is a leaf that looks half-folded, like an open book. This leaf has up to six very sensitive trigger hairs on each half. If an insect triggers more than two hairs, the leaf snaps shut, trapping the prey. Digestion of the victim usually takes three to five days. Another form of active trap uses suction. This suits carnivorous plants that live in ponds and lakes. A modified leaf traps air underwater by growing into a bladder shape. It has a kind of trapdoor on one side, triggered by sensitive hairs. When the hairs are tickled by passing prey, the trapdoor springs open, sucking water and the prey inside the bladder.

Key to plate

1: Common bladderwort
Utricularia macrorhiza
Length: up to 6¹/₂ feet/2 meters
(a) Flower (b) Stem and bladder traps
This plant grows in ponds and traps water creatures, such as water fleas. Each plant has thousands of traps, but no roots. Traps are usually only 3 millimeters long, but some species have traps that are ¹/₂ inch/1.2 centimeters long and can catch tadpoles.

2: Common sundew
Drosera rotundifolia
Height: 8 inches/20 centimeters
Leaf
This plant is now rarely seen, since so many bogs have been drained. Once struggling flies are stuck to its gluey leaves, the red, stalked glands push them into the center, where they are suffocated by liquid and their inner parts converted to a nutritious soup, absorbed by the leaf. Most of the two hundred species are found in western Australia.

3: Portuguese dewy sundew
Drosophyllum lusitanicum
Height: 16 inches/40 centimeters
Leaves
This rare shrub grows near the western part of the Mediterranean Sea in cork oak woodlands.

4: Rajah pitcher plant
Nepenthes rajah
Height: up to 10 feet/3 meters
Pitcher and leaf
The rajah pitcher plant has the largest pitchers of all—the size of a rugby ball—and is reputed to trap rats. It grows only on Mount Kinabalu, the tallest mountain in Borneo, and on one mountain nearby.

5: Cobra pitcher plant
Darlingtonia californica
Height: 16–33 cinches/ 40–85 centimeters
The cobra pitcher plant grows in the Sierra Nevada, in California. Flies landing on its red tongue follow a nectar trail to a hole underneath the domed, windowed "head." When they fly up toward the light coming through the head, they are trapped.

6: Venus flytrap
Dionaea muscipula
Leaf diameter: 8 inches/20 centimeters
There is only one species of Venus flytrap, which is found in the wild only in bogs near Wilmington, North Carolina. They usually trap and digest flies, but sometimes catch small frogs.

7: Common butterwort
Pinguicula vulgaris
Height: 6 inches/15 centimeters
The leaves of this plant attract, trap, and digest midges and mosquitoes. Around eighty species of butterwort are known from Europe, North America, and Asia, but most are in Mexico. When the leaves are added to milk, they separate it into curds (used to make butter) and whey.

1a 1b 2 3 4 5 6 7

Environment: Mangrove Forests

Mangrove forests are made up by trees and shrubs that grow in tropical and subtropical salt water between the high- and low-tide marks. They occur where flat, fertile tropical land meets the ocean—around 25 degrees latitude on either side of the Equator in Central and South America, the Caribbean, and Southeast Asia, and along the eastern and western coasts of Africa and the northern coasts of Australia. Mangrove swamps are hot, wet, and inhospitable. They often share their territory with saltwater crocodiles and mosquitoes.

Mangroves have a number of adaptations to deal with their harsh environment. Because the soil in swamps is salty, mangrove roots are largely impermeable, so they can limit the amount of salt water getting in. Some roots, such as those of the red mangrove tree, are infused with a substance called suberin, which acts as an extremely effective salt filter.

The swamp floors of mangrove environments also contain very little oxygen, which the underground tissue of plants needs for respiration (a chemical reaction to get energy needed to live). This means that the mangrove root system needs to take up oxygen from the atmosphere. Some swamp dwellers, like the red mangrove, have stilt roots, which can absorb oxygen directly from the air through pores in their bark called lenticels. Others, like the black mangrove, have special roots called pneumatophores, which stick straight up into the air, like snorkels, allowing them to take in oxygen.

Perhaps mangroves' most remarkable adaptation is the way they protect the next generation. Most aquatic plants disperse their seeds by allowing them to float in the water and germinate when they find land. Mangrove swamps are too harsh an environment for this, so the seed, once fertilized, germinates while still attached to the parent, either inside the fruit or out through its side. The seedling, called a propagule, will then detach itself and drop into the water, where it can survive for up to a year before taking root.

The dense, far-reaching root systems of mature mangrove forests offer protection from storms and tidal surges because they are adapted to absorb and dissipate energy from water. They also provide a vital habitat for oysters, crabs, and other species. Unfortunately, they also make ideal shrimp farms, and up to 20 percent of the world's mangrove forests appear to have been lost between 1980 and 2010, largely due to farming.

Key to plate

1: **Black mangrove**
Avicennia germinans
Height: 10 feet/3 meters

2: **Sundri tree**
Heritiera fomes
Height: 82 feet/25 meters

3: **Nipa palm**
Nypa fruticans
Height: 30 feet/9 meters

4: **Loop-root mangrove**
Rhizophora mucronata
Height: 115 feet/35 meters

5: **Red mangrove**
Rhizophora mangle
Height: 66 feet/20 meters

BOTANICUM

Library

Index

Curators

Katie Scott is illustrator of the best-selling *Animalium,* which was chosen as the 2014 London *Sunday Times* Children's Book of the Year.
She studied illustration at the University of Brighton and is inspired by the elaborate paintings of Ernst Haeckel.

Kathy Willis has spent the past twenty-five years researching and teaching at Cambridge and Oxford Universities. She is the director of science at the Royal Botanic Gardens, Kew, and as Professor of Biodiversity at the University of Oxford.
She lives in Oxford with her three children, two rabbits, one gecko, one dog, and a long-suffering husband.

To Learn More

ARKive
A compendium of life on Earth created by Wildscreen, a conservation organization based in England.
www.arkive.org

Botanical Society of Britain and Ireland
Advances the study and enjoyment of wild plants and supports their conservation in Britain and Ireland.
www.bsbi.org.uk

British Bryological Society
Information and resources for the study of British mosses and liverworts
rbg-web2.rbge.org.uk/bbs/bbs.htm

British Mycological Society
Enter the world of fungal biology research, conservation, and education.
www.britmycolsoc.org.uk

Grow Wild
Take part in the U.K.'s biggest-ever wild flower campaign, bringing people together to transform local spaces with native, pollinator-friendly wild flowers and plants.
www.growwilduk.com

The Linnean Society
The world's oldest active biological society. Online collections for research and educational resources. Learn about Carl Linnaeus and taxonomy.
www.linnean.org

Plantlife
An organization advocating for the conservation of wildflowers, plants, and fungi
www.theplantlist.org

Royal Botanic Gardens, Kew
Learn about Kew's scientists' work around the globe, including detailed profiles of four hundred species.
www.kew.org
www.kew.org/science-conservation
www.kew.org/kew-science/
people-and-data/resources-
and-databases

Royal Horticultural Society
The world's leading gardening charity, providing information and events on horticulture
www.rhs.org.uk

The Woodland Trust
Explore the British woodlands.
www.woodlandtrust.org